HOW TO PODCAST 2016:

Four Simple Steps to Broadcast your Message to the Entire Connected Planet ... even if You don't Know Where to Start

PAUL COLLIGAN

http://www.HowToPodcastBook.com

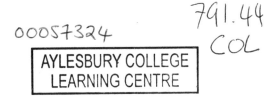
Copyright © 2016 Colligan.com, Inc.
All rights reserved.
ISBN: 1522995560
ISBN-13: 978-1522995562

About The Author

Paul Colligan helps others leverage technology to expand their reach and revenue, with reduced stress and no drama. He does this with a lifestyle and business designed to tackle the challenges and opportunities of today's ever-changing information economy. If you are looking for titles, Paul is a husband, father, eight time best-selling author, podcaster, keynote speaker, executive consultant, and the CEO of Colligan.com. He lives in Portland, Oregon with his wife and daughters and enjoys theater, music, great food and travel.

Paul believes in building systems and products that work for the *user* — not vice versa. With that focus, he has played a key role in the launch of dozens of successful internet products that have garnered tens of millions of visitors in traffic, and dollars in revenue. Previous projects have included work with The Pulse Network, Traffic Geyser, Rubicon International, Piranha Marketing, Microsoft and Pearson Education. In addition, he's helped dozens of authors launch their books and become best-sellers on Amazon, he's helped podcasters get to Number One on iTunes, and has been the secret weapon behind millions of video views on YouTube. Paul's topics of passion include podcasting, new media content creation, multicasting, product development, and lifestyle design.

Paul's unique take on the internet can be seen and heard on web shows, including The Podcast Report. It can be read in many books, including the Kindle Bestsellers *Cross Channel Social Media Marketing*, *How To Podcast 2015* and *YouTube Strategies 2015*. His work has been featured in several publications, including The Huffington Post and The Net Effect.

He is a popular speaker on internet technology topics, and has presented at events around the world including BlogWorld and New Media Expo, The European Business Podcasting Summit, Google Tech Talks, MacWorld, Social Media Success Summit, Inbound Marketing Summit, Social Media Marketing World and Microsoft TechEd.

If you are interested in his latest projects and his thoughts on podcasting, visit http://www.PaulColligan.com.

Table of Contents

PART 1 - HOW I PODCAST

About This Book

My name is Paul Colligan, and I've been in podcasting pretty much since day one. I love this space and I love training others on how to succeed in it. I have hundreds of students with millions of downloads who've seen success, ranging from a number one position in iTunes to simply making their Mom proud. I consider myself to be one of podcasting's biggest fans.

This isn't my first run at this. I already have two popular books about podcasting — *The Business Podcasting Bible* (released in 2006) and *Podcast Strategies* (released four years ago to a number one ranking in seven different countries). I still love both of these books and all that they represent, but they basically assume that you already know what podcasting is, and that you want to do more with it. This is, in fact, the updated version of my *How To Podcast 2015* book.

For almost ten years, I've been telling myself that I shouldn't do a "how-to" podcast book. I always believed there were people addressing this part of the process better than me, and I always thought that I should keep people focused on the revenue and monetization side of podcasting (my favorite parts). But this simple problem kept popping up:

People just kept making this more complicated than it needed to be. As a result, ten years later, some people aren't podcasting because they believe it's too complicated. This has to stop.

I can't stand unnecessary complication. It's a waste of all of our time.

Sometimes I wonder how much money has been made by making podcasting more complicated than it needs to be.

You only have so many hours in the day, and you don't need to waste them trying to understand someone's 200-page, overly complicated explanation of a much simpler process — especially if you're not looking to make a complicated podcast. I won't even get me started on a 20-part video series or a weekend-long boot camp. It's just not that complicated.

Is this book the whole story on podcasting? No. As the title states, this is a book on How To Podcast — and it is explained in four simple steps.

NOTE: THIS IS NOT A TECHNICAL BOOK, NOR IS IT FOR THE TECHNICALLY MINDED.

When it comes down to it, podcasting is about content, not technology. This is a book for the more novice user who likes podcasts, and wants to take a chance at producing one for themselves or for their company. If you're looking for a highly technical book, please put this one down. Don't worry, we'll talk about the tech — it just won't be the focus, because it shouldn't be the focus. I hope that's okay with you.

This is also not a "How to Make Money in Podcasting" or a "How to Market Your Podcast" book. Instead it is, quite simply, *How To Podcast* — and in four simple steps, no less. Of course, you're free to go on to any of those other topics (and I'd be thrilled to help you with some of them) once you're done with this short book.

This is in fact a brief guide on how I, personally, produce podcasts.

It's four steps .... really. That's it.

And this book explains them all.

Thanks for picking it up.

The Bonuses

As you might have read in the description for this book, I have a number of bonuses for you, from different companies who would love to have your podcasting business — be it technology, training, etc. They are all included with your little investment in this book. The goal is to give you the opportunity to earn back the amount that you spent on this volume many times over. I'm proud to say, that goal has been accomplished.

You can skip ahead to the bonus chapter for a quick peek right now if you want.

Register This Book / About Short Links

But you didn't just buy a book...

The nature of technology is that everything changes. At some point, a service I recommend in this book might have its price or its features changed, or it could become more complicated than it needs to be. I want to do what I can to protect you from that happening. We're going to do that (to the best of my capabilities) in these two ways:

First, I'm going to ask that you register this book. By registering this book, I'll be able to keep you up to date by email on any major changes that you need to know about. If I make a change to the book, I'll make sure you have a digital copy.

To register this book, visit http://HowToPodcastBook.com/Register

In addition to keeping you up to date with all of the changes that are going on, I'll also give you access to a special bonus pack of how-to videos, additional content and more. You'll only get these when you register the book. It's my way of saying thanks — and making this "more" than a book (regardless of whether it's the electronic or the paper edition).

Second, I'm also going to make (nearly) all of the links in this book special shortlinks — quick hyperlinks which redirect you immediately to webpages — that I can update to redirect you in case anything changes. You'll notice every link in this book is in this format: http://h2plink.com/X — where X is the recommended resource. For example, http://h2plink.com/Paul is my blog.

This isn't to make things more complicated — it's actually to protect you on this journey. If there is something that I write about or mention that has changed dramatically, and you need to know about it, the link will take you to a quick explanation before it takes you to the main site.

My promise to you is that I'll keep this book updated for the entire year. Register the book and you'll find out when the next updated version is released — I'll make sure you get that at a ridiculously good rate, too.

Fair enough? Let's get to work!

Man, This Book is Short!

Yes, I purposely kept this book short so that you could finish it quickly and get to work. I don't want you debating platforms or microphone types. I want you broadcasting your message to the world.

Here's the thing: your first podcast will be your worst podcast. And the sooner you get that one recorded and published, the sooner you'll get better at it. Once that happens, it might be time to look at elements which are a bit more complicated — but between now and then, let's get your first podcast LIVE.

Paul, I Found A Typo — Or A Mistake — Or, You're Grammar Weren't Good!

I bet you did. Typos are going to happen. It's actually one of the reasons I prefer podcasting over book authoring — nobody knows when I'm spelling things wrong in front of a microphone!

If you find something that needs a fix, point it out on the Facebook page (mentioned below) and I just might give you a shout-out for your awesome grammarizing (yeah, that's a word) in the next release of this book.

Affiliate Disclaimer

I create commercial content that helps pay the bills. I am what many call an information marketer.

Often, I am the provider and owner of the products and services that I recommend. Being in this business provides me such a wonderful opportunity. It's part of how I pay those bills.

Occasionally, the companies that provide the products and services I recommend compensate me. It is sometimes direct, sometimes indirect — but it is there.

If this offends you, no problem; this isn't content for you. Return this book. We can still be friends.

At all times, I only recommend products I use — or would tell my Mom to use. You have my promise there.

Let's Continue the Conversation

The internet continues to change on a regular basis, and I can pretty much promise you that once we send this book to be distributed, many of these changes will have already kicked in. The best way to stay informed on the changes that impact you is to register your book at http://HowToPodcastBook.com/Register, but here are some other options as well:

I set up a Facebook page specifically for this book at http://www.Facebook.com/HowToPodcast. When you launch your podcast as a result of this book, make sure you post it there, too. You deserve the attention and acclaim that we'll be sending your way when you do.

My blog is online at http://www.PaulColligan.com — drop by and say hi!

In terms of social networking, you can find me in all the usual places:

- http://PaulColligan.com/Twitter
- http://PaulColligan.com/Facebook
- http://PaulColligan.com/Instagram
- http://PaulColligan.com/Pinterest
- http://PaulColligan.com/YouTube

Thanks for buying the book! You won't regret it.

Paul Colligan
HowToPodcastBook@Gmail.com
Portland, Oregon
December 2015

HOW TO PODCAST

4 SIMPLE STEPS

1 MAKE DIGITAL MEDIA

2 PUT IT ONLINE

3 MAKE IT PODCAST READY

4 TELL THE WORLD

PODCAST DONE!

Wasn't that easy?

What is Podcasting?

Podcasting is, quite simply:

Audio or video made available online for easy on-demand consumption and/or subscription-based delivery.

That's it.

You were expecting more, weren't you? Others have certainly tried to make it out to be more than that. Of course, there are details and nuances, but that's podcasting in a nutshell.

Yes, it is simple — but there is power in simplicity.

That's it. The whole Apple, iTunes, iPad, iPhone podcasting thing — it's all possible because of the fact that it's *audio or video made available online for easy on-demand consumption and/or subscription-based delivery.*

But it's not just an Apple thing. What about the podcasts on a Google device, a Microsoft phone, a connected car stereo, or some other platform out there which supports podcasts? Those too are simply *audio or video made available online for both easy on-demand consumption and/or subscription-based delivery.*

One single podcast will work on any device looking to access your content. You don't need to make things specifically for an iPad, Android device, connected car stereo, or any other device or platform.

Once your podcast is up and running, it works on any device, and for anyone looking to connect with your content. In that way, it is just like radio or television. It makes no difference if the listener gets your content on a Sony or a Hitachi device. What really matters, in fact, is that they *can* get your content.

Why do others make it so complicated?

There are a number of theories as to why some have tried to make podcasting more complicated than the definition above. They range from conspiracy level: *"they can't charge you as much once you realize how easy it is"* — to the more human explanation of: *"some people are so excited by the tech that they want to share every single element of it with you — even if you don't need it."*

When I was first putting this book together, I posted this definition online to a few podcaster sites to see what they thought. If someone had a simpler way of explaining the process, I certainly wanted to share it with you.

I was able to refine the definition a bit, and I'm happy with how we've defined it. But trust me on this — there are a lot of people with definitions much more complicated than mine.

The reasons people have for making podcasting complicated don't really matter. This book is about making it simple so that in the end, you can get your podcast up and running quickly.

I'll say it one more time — podcasting is, simply: *audio or video made available online for easy on-demand consumption and/or subscription-based delivery.*

That's the definition used in this book and the basis for the process we outline in this book. It is the *process* that is going to get you up and running with your podcast in no time at all.

Let's break down our definition and look at it with a bit more focus and clarity:

Audio or Video ...

Almost all audio or video media is digital now, and conversion is easy for the few pieces that aren't yet digitized. The important benefit of digital media is that it's stored on a hard drive or a chip somewhere — not in a warehouse or on store shelves with a distinct physical copy for each and every person. The same scale that quickly made Apple the biggest retailer of music is now the force behind *your* message. How cool is that?

As technology has advanced, digital media has improved as well. This means that the files are getting smaller and smaller in size, making them easier to send over the internet. The quality is getting higher and higher, meaning they look and sound better. Oh, the joys of technology!

....Made Available Online....

Because your media is placed online, it's accessible to anyone with a connection to the internet. Because the internet is almost ubiquitous now, accessing your content isn't a question of "Apple vs. Windows" or "iPhone vs. Android" — it's available anytime, anywhere, to anyone who knows where to find it.

....For Easy On-Demand Consumption....

Yes, it needs to be made easily accessible. Fortunately, that is incredibly simple to do with the existing podcasting and traditional web infrastructure. The great part is that you pay NO licensing fees to make your media available to the world, and everything that you're going to need in order to achieve that global exposure — at minimal cost — is included in this book.

Okay, so there are no licensing fees for podcasting, but what does it cost to make your audio and video available to the world? There are options to distribute this easily-accessible content to the world for less than the price of a large pizza each month. We'll discuss that in more depth in Step Two. You might notice in our bonus section that one of the biggest names in podcasting is going to give you your first month for free, just for picking up this book.

....And/or Subscription-Based Delivery.

Finally, your content needs a subscription option, so that when someone finds out they really like your message, they can subscribe. This feature alone remains one of the biggest strengths of podcasting. With subscription-based delivery, every time you release a new episode, your subscribers will get it automatically, 100% spam-free. This is not just an iPhone or Smart TV feature, nor is it owned by Apple — this is, quite simply, the backbone of podcasting....and you can set it up very quickly.

12

Not everyone uses the subscription element of podcasting, and that's unfortunate. Once someone has found content they like from a source that they trust, it is imperative to make sure they understand that they can get new episodes automatically — usually with just the click of a button.

Is That It?

Is that everything? Can it really be so simple?

Yes. What's more, this book will cover EVERYTHING you need to get your podcast up and running. We'll even explain it to you in just four simple steps.

If you're looking for something more complicated, you're not going to find it here. I hope that's okay ;-)

Let's get to it!

Step 1 - Make Digital Media

First things first - podcasting isn't only audio; it can also be video or even PDF files. Audio is currently the most popular form of podcasting, but video is quickly catching up. Distribution of other media files, like PDF, is possible, but currently has a limited appeal and audience.

What is the difference between podcasting and digital media online? In short, podcasting provides a digital "wrapper" around your online media that makes it accessible to all podcasting clients, enabling extra benefits like syndication and subscription. We'll discuss those in detail in the next chapters. The first step is simply to make the media, so that we can put a podcast wrapper around it.

It might seem a bit redundant to say "digital" media since almost all media is digital nowadays, but I wanted to start at the very beginning and stay true to my promise — that this stuff is newbie-friendly. I'll be honest, I've even had a few people take existing audio tapes and make them into a podcast. Yes, this is possible. In this chapter I'm also going to explain how to make digital media without a microphone or a camera.

With that said and done, this book is going to be focused primarily on audio, since at the time of writing, the majority of podcasting is done using audio.

Digital Audio in Two Steps

In the production of digital audio, the first step requires recording and editing your audio, with the best possible quality, onto your phone or your computer. After you are done with every single aspect of your audio — including production, editing and enhancing — you will then need to convert it into an MP3 file that is podcast-compatible.

That's basically it — now, the specifics...

Is All Digital Media a Podcast?

You may be asking yourself, "What's the difference between a podcast and other online media, such as a YouTube video or a media file on my website?"

Great question.

At the core of it, any digital media you create can be used to produce YouTube videos, CDs, streaming radio shows and more. It is the same media — it's just what you do with the media that makes it a podcast. In terms of file format, it is all the same thing.

So in this step, forget about podcasting. You are simply creating digital media to use any way you want. I call that process "multicasting," and it's a big deal — but just not the focus of this book.

Making Digital Media Right Now

The chances are very high that you have a smartphone — you might even be reading this book on one right now. Honestly, that's all you need to make a digital recording. I have a podcast that I record almost entirely on my phone when I get stuck in traffic. More details about that particular podcast can be found here:

http://h2plink.com/ThinkingOutLoud

Yes, all I need to do to make that podcast happen is to talk into my phone. I usually record while driving and running errands. I use a pair of earbuds, which I picked up for $9.99, simply because that's all I tend to have in the car with me when I record an episode.

I told you: this doesn't need to be complicated.

Believe it or not, there are a number of surprisingly good smartphone programs that record audio — so many, in fact, that I hesitate to list any specific one here. However, here is a great combo microphone-and-software package that works on both iPhone and Android devices.

It's called the iRig Mic Cast:

http://h2plink.com/PhoneMic

Will you have a high-fidelity, perfect-sounding podcast using your phone? No. But you don't always need a high-fidelity, perfect-sounding podcast. Sometimes, good enough is good enough. I've had clients whose podcast episodes have hundreds of thousands of downloads, and they were recorded with even less.

If you don't have a smartphone, or don't really want to use one to record your content, there are plenty of options to use your computer as well. In addition to your computer, you will need a USB computer microphone and an audio recording program.

My favorite computer microphone right now is the "Nessie" by Blue, which works on both Apple and Windows machines. That could change at any time (my preference I mean — the microphone will always work on both operating systems), but the following link will always take you to a great option (i.e. my favorite microphone at the time).

http://h2plink.com/Nessie

Another option is the very powerful iRig iMic HD

http://h2plink.com/iRigiMicHD

Some of the computer microphones today record surprisingly well and can help you sound a lot better than you might think.

My favorite audio recording program for the computer is Audacity. It's free and it also works on both Apple and Windows machines. Yes, you read that right.

http://h2plink.com/Audacity

There are, of course, plenty of other choices. The beauty of this space is that there are lots of ways to record audio.

Remember: don't get lost in all of the options. Again, millions of hours of podcasts have been consumed with less technology than I've listed above. Trust me — you don't need to make this complicated.

For a video tutorial of recording audio on the iRig Mic Cast, visit this link:

http://h2plink.com/AudioOnMicCast

To see how I record "Thinking Out Loud" using nothing but my iPhone, visit this link:

http://h2plink.com/HowIRecordTOL

Here's another bonus video for you: "How To Record And Edit Audio on Your Computer with Audacity and the Nessie USB Microphone"

http://h2plink.com/AudacityNessie

Audio Recording, Without Fancy Equipment or Software

As I write these few paragraphs, I can already hear in my head some pundits in this space composing their rebuttal to what I am about to recommend. However, it all goes back to that simple question: "Why do they have to make it more complicated than it needs to be?"

There are a number of companies that provide conference-call services for little to no cost, and many of them will record the call as well. One easy way to record podcast audio, including interviews with participants in other locations, is to use one of these services.

At the time of writing, UberConference (http://h2plink.com/UberConference) has a free service with great audio. This option is subject to change, but even their $10-per-month offering is currently well worth your money. You simply call into the service and chat as usual, and the system records the call for you.

You may also be wondering: "Doesn't audio recorded on a phone bridge *sound* like audio recorded on a phone bridge?" Yes, it does — but that doesn't always matter. The very popular and excellent "I Love Marketing" podcast (http://h2plink.com/ILoveMarketing) gets thousands of downloads a day, and is often recorded in this very manner. Dean Jackson, the show's co-host, calls it the "No-Click Podcast."

Editing Digital Media

So, you've made some digital media — and it isn't perfect. There is a whole debate about what is "good enough" in terms of quality, but we won't deal with that here. Many of you will still want to edit after you've created your audio, and that's understandable.

Fortunately, many of the programs used to record digital media can also be used to edit digital media. If you think of them like a word processor for media, you'll be in a good place. Put in your initial content, then edit it so that it's as clean and mistake-free as possible.

Audacity, the company I recommended earlier, is also a great, *simple* platform for editing audio. There are lots of options, but I like going with simple — and, yes, it is what my team uses to edit ALL of my podcasts right now. The simpler the program, the easier it is going to be to edit. You're not going for major awards here; your goal is to get your point across.

Is the volume not quite right? Is there a wacky audio hum that you need to get rid of? We'll cover a very easy solution to that problem. Pay special attention to everything I have to say about the cloud solution Auphonic a little later on.

Another possibility for getting your audio edited is to outsource it. "Isn't that incredibly expensive?" It can be — but there are some interesting options to consider in the offshore world. Take a look at Fiverr (http://h2plink.com/Fiverr) and search for "audio editing." The work you can get done for just $5 is quite surprising. *Obviously, buyer-beware for any kind of service like this.* That being said, it is still worth looking at. Other options that are a little less "bottom of the barrel" include eLance (http://h2plink.com/Elance) and People Per Hour (http://h2plink.com/PeoplePerHour).

New: Editing Audio With Ferrite

A new option in the audio editing and recording world (on iOS, at least) is an app called "Ferrite" from a company called, of all things "Wooji Juice."

http://h2plink.com/Ferrite

Two things make Ferrite worth mentioning: 1) It's a complete recording and editing solution for iOS (and only iOS at the time of writing) and 2) It will export your projects in an uncompressed format directly into the Auphonic App for leveling, tagging, etc.

This means you can record, edit and publish a Podcast using nothing but an iOS device. While this might be a bit tight on an iPhone, the same iPad Pro I type this into can become a fairly complete audio Podcasting machine.

I will probably be moving my workflow to recording and editing in Ferrite and then moving to Auphonic for post production. If you register this book and I come up with a process, I'll make sure to keep you in the loop.

There are several microphones that record great digital sound directly into iOS devices, including the iRig iMic HD and the Blu Nessie (when connected with the USB). Combine this with Ferrite and things get interesting indeed.

http://h2plink.com/iRigiMicHD

http://h2plink.com/Nessie

Note: At the time this was written, there is still no easy way to record an interview from another program such as Skype or FaceTime (on a phone or tablet device), so if you are getting content from external programs, this is not the solution for you.

Does Editing Make Your Content Better?

One thing that traps many podcasters is the editing process. They spend a few minutes recording the content, but then they get caught up in the cycle of editing, and are not willing to release the final product until it is perfect.

Striving for perfection can really work against you in podcasting. Your main goal as a podcaster is to get your message out, not sound like you were recorded in an expensive studio. Sure, you don't want to burst audience eardrums with an overly dramatic sneeze. But you should realize that the occasional "um" or pause just proves that you're a human.

Making Better-Sounding and Better-Looking Media

Despite what you might hear from the microphone manufacturers and others who might benefit from making things sound more complicated and more expensive than they really are — sounding good has nothing to do with the microphone.

90% of getting a good sound depends on two things: the environment in which you are recording, and how close your mouth is to the microphone when you record. All you need to do is use a decent microphone, place it near your lips and record in a good environment, and you are almost there.

What makes a good environment for recording is pretty obvious. It shouldn't be noisy where you are recording. You should also try to keep noise from bouncing around the room. The same acoustics that motivate you to put carpet down and add some furniture in a room apply to the space where you record. YouTube is a great source of videos on this process, if you need more help.

If soundproofing is not an option, you can always put your microphone in a box like this one:

http://h2plink.com/MicBox

In the worst-case scenario, you can do the very thing BBC war correspondents did during World War II: record with a blanket over your head and the microphone. Don't knock it — it really works! I've recorded more than a dozen episodes of different shows using this technique, including (ironically) an episode recorded at 2 a.m. in a London hotel room.

Auphonic

Auphonic is my podcasting secret weapon. In short, this is the tool I use to optimize my sound and convert it to MP3 format. I highly recommend you do the same.

Basically, I used to spend an hour or so optimizing my audio manually. Now, I just run it through Auphonic and it sounds better than it ever used to.

While Auphonic doesn't fix everything, it does an amazing job and is definitely worth a look.

Video - How I Optimize my Audio and Convert it to MP3 Using Auphonic

http://h2plink.com/AuphonicVIdeo

Lossless files

I won't go into the technical details here, but trust me on this next tip. This comes from almost a decade of cumulative experience from both my students and myself.

When you create your audio files and manage them throughout all of the editing process, keep everything in a "lossless" file format. This usually means a ".WAV" or ".AIFF" file.

Why? When you edit compressed media, it always loses a bit of sound quality in the process. If you don't want that problem, you can get around it by editing your files in a lossless format.

Once you're done, as the FINAL step, convert it into the MP3 file that your podcasting audience is looking for. If you're looking for specifics, I like using **128 kbps MP3 files** — it will be an option in whatever audio program you are using.

Making Media Without a Camera or Microphone

I've had plenty of people ask me over the years about using a voice-to-text program to take existing text-only articles or blog posts and convert them into an audio podcast. While this is technically possible, it's just a really bad idea. The software just isn't sophisticated enough yet to convey what you are trying to say in the way that you want to say it. And, let's face it, it sounds like a computer reading an article — nobody wants that.

However, your podcast does not necessarily have to be in your own personal speaking voice.

One option is to outsource the recording of the podcast to voice talent. Basically, this just involves having someone else read your words. It's expensive, and involves a few more steps than just clicking "record," but it works. At the time of writing, I know of at least one podcast in the Top 20 on iTunes that follows this very method.

If you are thinking about producing video and the thought of dealing with lights, HD cameras and skin blemishes makes you a little queasy, don't worry — there is the whole world of "screencasting" to explore. This is basically just video content recorded from your computer screen, often in the form of Powerpoint or Keynote slideshows. Just because people want to look at something while they listen to your podcast doesn't mean it has to be your face.

Another option I recommend is just to GET OVER IT. Part of what makes podcasting so powerful is that it's you, conveying your message, in your voice. Let's be honest, you aren't perfect — and any podcast you produce will reflect that fact. However, when is the last time you heard something "perfect" and weren't a little suspicious? Be you — you're the best podcaster you've got.

For example, Michael Stelzner of Social Media Examiner, does a podcast five days a week without ever talking into a microphone. Remember, you always have options.

Warning: Make Sure You Are Legal

This section could be a whole book, but the bottom line is this: *don't ever use audio, video or other recorded sounds or images made by someone else in your podcast without being 100% sure that you have the full legal rights to do so.*

You may think you're so small that it doesn't matter, or you may have heard the term "fair use" and think it applies to you. It doesn't.

I'm no lawyer, and I certainly don't attempt to play one on TV, but believe me — using someone else's content in your podcast is a quick way to get yourself into a lot of trouble. Without going into details, the downloadable nature of podcasting, combined with the international availability of the internet, makes this stuff very tempting to lawyers looking for easy prey.

In addition to being a really bad idea, it's pretty slimy in nature. You wouldn't want someone using your stuff without your permission, would you?

I won't go any deeper into this than what I've written above, but I know podcasters who have gotten into trouble and paid painful legal fees because they thought this issue didn't apply to them. It applies to them — and it applies to you.

I should also point out that if you have content created or edited for you by someone else that contains copyrighted content, you're just as liable. If someone tells you that the audio or video they've created for you is free of copyrights and restrictions, it's a smart move to ask for some documented proof. The good ones will be willing to provide it to you.

On a side note: If you want to put some theme music into your podcast, I've partnered with LegalPodastMusic.com to give you a great deal.

People Come for the Podcast Content, They Stay for the Podcast Voice

This section header is a loose paraphrase of Merlin Mann and Dan Benjamin from the 5by5 network (http://h2plink.com/5by5), but it's an important point nonetheless.

Their idea is simple: the power of podcasting does not lie in the quality of the recording or the technology behind your MP3 file — it's in the power of the ideas and thoughts being communicated by the host.

To dig a little deeper, it's not even really what you say, but how you say it, that keeps people coming back. It's your voice that makes your podcast special, so make sure you spend more time on that than on anything else.

What About GarageBand, Adobe Audition or [insert fancypants audio editing program here]...?

There are plenty of great options for recording and editing digital media, and there have been plenty of books written and training programs designed to teach you how to do them...but that's not the point of this book.

You are free to try any of these platforms and options. But you should realize that expensive audio programs will not make you a better podcaster any more than an expensive knife will make you a better chef.

Now, if you are already familiar with one of these programs, go ahead and use it — there's no need to waste any time learning something new. I just want to prevent the pain for someone out there who thinks that they need to master complicated software in order to share their message with the world.

That's It?

Yes, that's it. Step 1 is as simple as talking into your phone...and as complicated as you want to make it beyond that. Editing can be done quickly and easily, with powerful online tools like Auphonic doing all the heavy lifting.

Are you ready to take action? Go for it! Need a little more? Watch the videos we've mentioned to get all the specifics. Either way, you are ready for Step 2 — so let's turn our attention to putting your media online.

Step 2 - Put It Online

Once you've made your digital media, you need to place it online. You should use a service that can distribute it to people around the world when they request it, and provide any podcast-specific services, if and when they are needed. This can be ridiculously cheap. You just need to have the right mindset and find the right partners. We'll set you up with those here — and even get you a free month with one of our favorite services.

Be aware: there are some requirements specific to podcasting that prevent you from putting your podcast just anywhere — but don't worry, you have lots of options.

How Media Gets Online

For those unfamiliar with the process, let me take a few minutes to highlight a few different ways you can get your media online.

The easiest way is usually to "upload" your MP3 file through the web interface of your media host. There are also some automated tools, like Auphonic, that will do the file transfer for you automatically as part of their process.

View the following video to see how easy it is to put your podcast media online using Libsyn.com, the host I use and recommend: (http://h2plink.com/Libsyn).

Free Video: Putting Podcast Media Online

http://h2plink.com/PutMediaOnline

Is Online the Same Thing as "The Cloud?"

I've seen a funny t-shirt that says *"No one really knows what the cloud is."* I hate to make complicated things too simple, but the "cloud" is simply a hard drive or computer attached to the internet that you don't have to monitor or maintain.

This is exactly what you want for your online podcasting media: you want it on someone else's internet-connected hard drive, and you don't want to worry about a thing once you've put it there. In the cloud, your data is always available and accessible whenever and wherever you need it.

The beautiful thing about the cloud is that it always acts the same, regardless of what time it is and whether or not you happen to be connected to the internet. This is the kind of service your podcast deserves.

Remember, our goal is to keep it simple and get things done. Any podcast host we recommend in this book will meet your needs and will be, for all intents and purposes, a "cloud" service.

The Right Mindset / Can I Use Free Hosting?

All hosts are no more the same than are all cars.

Many of the hosting companies that offer "unlimited" hosting often have tiny little fine print, which basically says that online media files aren't included in their service. Also, they often host media in a way that iTunes will simply reject.

In some cases, you won't get caught and iTunes won't care. But if your show ends up doing a lot of business, you could get shut down quickly. Nothing is worse than seeing your podcast finally get the attention it deserves, and then finding out that your host has shut you down as a result.

In terms of "free hosting," you, my friend, can do whatever you want. However, the old phrase that "you get what you pay for" is as true of podcast hosting as it is anywhere else. You want a partner who can handle the traffic when it comes, and can make and keep the big players happy.

Even though it's not free, reliable media hosting does not need to be expensive. There is a whole industry of media hosting that is extremely affordable, with some options starting as low as $5 a month. Your podcast hosting doesn't need to be a burden or an out-of-control expense — but you should pay a few bucks to do it right.

The Right Partners

There are two kinds of partners out there in the podcasting space: the *technology* partners (media hosts, feed builders, etc.), and what we'll call *marketing* partners. A marketing partner claims they will not only help you make your podcast, but also promote it, get advertisers for it and more. You need a good technology partner, without a doubt — but I strongly encourage you to consider whether or not your podcast actually needs a marketing partner.

Technology partners have come a long way in the last ten years. Now, there are a number of great candidates who meet the podcast hosting requirements I write about and even provide feed-authoring services as well. One of the best things about not being first at this game is that you don't need to make the mistakes others have made. Join up with a partner that has already done what you are hoping to do. I list a few excellent partners in the next section of this chapter.

In terms of finding a marketing partner company, I recommend that you stay away from them. In short, I've never seen one with a model that works. I'm not going to name names here, but if you find a company that seems to be offering you the world and claims they will bring you an audience, sell advertising on your show and more, please know that in my experience, I've never seen it happen successfully — and I doubt you will either.

What is a Byte-Range Request, and Does it Matter?

ATTENTION: NERD ALERT — BUT THIS IS IMPORTANT

Apple now requires that servers serving media files have something called "byte-range requests" enabled. Make sure your podcast host has this feature — everyone we recommend in this book does.

Who We Recommend for Your Hosting Technology Partner

You want to put your media on a host specifically designed for podcasts. The only host I recommend now is Libsyn.com, which has prices as low as $5 a month (yes, you read that right) and can be found here:

http://h2plink.com/Libsyn

And, you can use the coupon code "Paul" to get your first month for free!

How good are they? Libsyn hosts ALL of my podcasts as well as the podcasts of all of my clients. At this point in the game there is simply no other choice. If something new pops up, I'll let you know (as long as you register your book).

How Can Unlimited Hosting Be Real?

I'm going to spend a paragraph or two dealing with an issue that any thinking person needs to examine. How can someone offer unlimited hosting for such low prices? Is it really unlimited? Can you trust it?

It's all about the math, and the economies of scale.

While no one can give you true unlimited hosting without losing money, especially at the rates some hosts charge, very few podcasts are capable of generating the kind of traffic that will cost the hosting company money. It's the same story when my teenage daughter uses about five minutes of her unlimited voice minutes plan on her phone during any given month (although texting is another story).

Essentially, hosting companies buy in bulk at a discount, and bank on the fact that very few podcasts are as popular as their creators want them to be. They make up their revenue in volume. However, some of my favorite associates and past students have been the exceptions to this rule, and many of the media hosts listed in this book are losing money on those podcasts every month.

So, while there are some podcasts that represent a monthly financial loss to any hosting company, there are still enough that don't — so they can afford to offer hosting at competitive prices and still make money.

Will we see unlimited hosting options forever? I'm betting yes, but I can't tell you for sure. Hosting and bandwidth are getting cheaper every day, so it would take significant industry changes for this option to die.

About Reporting And Statistics

There is a lot that can be said about reporting statistics, but we're keeping things simple here. In short, the way hosts traditionally manage and track files simply doesn't work in podcasting. There are plenty of articles about this fact online if you want to look for them.

What does this mean to you? Well, it means that you'll want reporting specifically designed for podcasting and the unique issues it brings to the table. Libsyn (http://h2plink.com/Libsyn), mentioned earlier, has a great reporting package included in their program. Another good option is the stats program offered by Blubrry (http://h2plink.com/Blubrry).

Many people who are making their first foray into the podcasting space are disappointed to realize how limited the podcasting stats actually are. The very nature of the downloadable media file delivered via a podcast means that you don't get information on how many times a specific file was downloaded, or if it was listened to, or even for how long it was listened to. No matter what you've heard, podcast reporting is limited to what was downloaded, where it was downloaded and what technologies were used in the process. This limitation is something all podcasters have to deal with, no matter how successful they are.

Again, this isn't something you need to worry about. The data you can get from podcast reporting is still phenomenal — it just may not be as complete as you had hoped.

One interesting thing to note about podcasting stats is that companies such as Stitcher (http://h2plink.com/Stitcher), which offer streaming services, can deliver a few more stats about your podcast, at least in terms of how it plays to their audience. The information that hosts like these provide is fascinating, but it hardly forms a complete picture.

What Happens if I Have to Change Media Hosts?

Common sense dictates that you should keep a backup of your podcast episodes, and I encouraged you to do that in Step 1. The worst-case scenario when changing hosts means you will have to take your archive, move it, and then point your podcast audience to the new host (more on that in the next section). Archive well, and the worst-case scenario can be navigated effortlessly.

This mobility illustrates the beauty of the podcasting infrastructure. You can pick up and move your podcast, just like you can pick up and move from one mobile phone company to another. If you've ever moved web hosting providers, you'll find that it is pretty much the same type of experience.

Pick a Host and Move On to the Next Chapter

That's all there is for Step 2. Pick a host that makes sense for you, get your media online, and then move on to the next chapter.

That's it!

Yes, that's it. Once you have your media online with a smart host, you're ready for the next step: making your content podcast-ready. You'll be surprised by how easy it is.

Step 3 - Make it Podcast-Ready

Now we're getting to the part that elevates this from simply creating online media to creating a podcast. A *podcast feed* is the heart of what makes it possible for you to podcast your media so people can subscribe to it. Like before, you'll need the right mindset and the right partners if you want to get it done quickly, without any tech worries or dramas.

Don't worry; we're not going to get too technical here. A feed is simply what you need to make your content podcast-ready. That's why I named this chapter after the end result, not the process. Another way to think of it is this: the feed contains all the directions that a podcast client (like the iPhone) needs to make it all work. They're pretty quick and easy to make, *if you do it right* — and this chapter explains how to do it.

Part of your podcast feed consists of data found in your album art information — which we'll also cover in this chapter.

This should be the shortest step of your podcasting journey. Your only job here is to pick the right partner for this process and then move on to your content production. If this isn't the shortest chapter in the book, or you spend any time worrying about this step, I've done something wrong.

How Does Online Media Become "Podcast-Ready?"

A little behind-the-scenes fact: podcast (RSS) feeds are in a file format called "XML". XML is something that is read only by computers and, as a result, should be generated, automatically, by a computer. Think of XML the same way you think of

"Postscript" — the file format your computer uses to tell the printer how to print something. *That's right: a Microsoft Word doc, a PDF viewer or any other file you send to the printer uses a special language only the geekiest of nerds know how to program in (and you probably didn't even know it existed).* Approach XML and your podcast feeds in the same way — it's something that computers do, not you.

So, we're going to find a computer to write your podcast's feed for you, so that you can worry about the content. Fair enough?

Once you finish the process of setting up a feed, it is truly a "set-it-and-forget-it" system, which you can leave alone and not worry about for a single moment, ever again. Once you've done this correctly, the world is automatically updated with everything they need to know about your podcast — including updates when new episodes are released.

If you're a bit more techie and you're wondering if feeds for blogs and feeds for podcasts are the same thing, the answer is: in many ways, yes. Feeds for podcasts have additional information related to the media attached, and have a few variables that allow *podcatchers* (such as iTunes) to give some content specifically related to podcasting.

What Does a Feed Look Like?

A feed file is accessible over the internet with a web address, usually in some version of the form: http://www.domain.com/feed.rss.

Straight, untranslated RSS is hard for a human to decipher, although some systems will produce a more human-friendly interpretation of an RSS feed. Such an approach is unnecessary from a technical standpoint, but it prevents some people from thinking that something is broken when they click on a URL associated with your podcast and see nothing but code.

Where Do Feeds Come From?

Feeds are basically produced in three different ways:

Option 1: *A number of podcasting hosts such as Libsyn generate your feed for you automatically.* If this is the path you choose, it is more than enough, and allows you to work on content instead of analyzing XML. I like this option a lot because, simply, it lets the computer do the stuff that computers are good at doing.

Option 2: *Most blogging platforms such as WordPress (http://h2plink.com/WordPress) generate basic RSS feeds by default.* Believe it or not, in most cases, the feed produced automatically by linking to a media file in your blog is enough to work with iTunes — although it is by no means optimized to deliver a great presentation. There are WordPress plugins you can use such as PowerPress (http://h2plink.com/PowerPress) that will refine the process slightly and allow you to deliver all of the information that iTunes is looking for.

Option 3: *The last option is to write the feed yourself.* I can't tell you how much I hate this approach. I find it to be the stuff bad science fiction stories are made of — when we do the work that the robots should be doing, the robots win.

In my opinion, you should no more write your own XML then you should write the Postscript file for the shopping list that you send to the printer. However, there are some control freaks who insist on doing it themselves, and occasionally there is a business reason for doing so (although this is a .01% kind of thing). If you believe you need to do this, I suggest two things: double check again that there isn't a tool which meets your needs, and don't let the person in charge of writing the code produce the content for your podcast.

In my batch of free videos associated with this book, you'll notice a video called "How A Podcast Host Makes My RSS So I Don't Have To" (http://h2plink.com/MakesMyRSS). That video walks you through the process I use for one of my podcasts.

Why iTunes Comes First in Podcast Feeds

If you're wondering how in the world you can make a single feed that works in iTunes, and in Stitcher, and for Microsoft machines, and for *the other 100 options that make podcasting so exciting*, I have some great news for you. Thanks to the beautiful work already done by Apple, the reality is simple:

All you need to do to make sure your podcast feed works everywhere is to make sure that it works on iTunes.

Every podcast client tracks and monitors what Apple is doing,

40

and makes sure that whatever you put in your feed (for the sake of Apple), works on their system as well.

Use this to your advantage and quickly make a feed that works on iTunes — and then get back to creating your content.

Why You *Must* Control Your Feed

The web address for your feed is how the world, and the podcast directories (more on that in the next chapter) know how to find you. If you suddenly have to change feeds, it's hard to let the world know you've done just that. Although there are ways to migrate one feed to another, it's very complicated, time consuming, not 100% effective, and rarely works as planned.

Think of your podcast feed in the same way that you think of your mobile phone number. Just as you should never sign up with a phone service provider who is vague about what happens to your number if you ever leave their service, never work with a feed provider who isn't crystal clear that *you own your feed* and can do what you want with it. When you own the phone number, you can hop from one provider to another without anyone having to know. Moving your podcast feed, should you ever need to, should be just as simple.

Many hosts give you the chance to use their service and link it with your domain, so you'd have a feed along the lines of: http://www.yourdomain.com/yourfeed.rss. This is the smartest move. Why? Because if you have to move from one host or service to another, the world doesn't need to know.

Obviously, if you're using a tool to create the feed on your own domain, you don't need to worry about this.

I'll be blunt: there are some providers who, once they create the feed for your show, own that feed (and host it on their own domain), which makes it almost impossible for you to ever leave them. Sometimes they do it on purpose, sometimes they are just being lazy. Either way it's a bad move, and you want to stay away from them. I have an alternative for you later in this chapter (Feedburner), but stay away from such providers if at all possible.

About Album Art (or Podcast Art)

Podcasting started because of the MP3 player, and from day one it mimicked the infrastructure already set in place for that platform to make things work smoothly. Things matched up pretty nicely and we never turned back. For a podcast, the terms are simply changed to "Show Title" instead of "Album Name", and what were once called "Tracks" are now called "Episodes." Yes, the average album might have 10 "episodes," but there is no set limit. So don't worry, nothing will break when you pass episode number 200.

When you open up any podcatching program (such as iTunes), you'll notice that all podcasts have square artwork to represent each podcast. This also comes from the MP3 player world, and is equivalent to "Album Art" in an MP3 player. Just like Taylor Swift's Album *1989* has a distinctive piece of album art, your podcast can have its own unique podcast art.

Podcast art should be square, simply because that's the format which the industry expects from albums. At the time of publication, iTunes wants your album art to be at least 1400 x 1400 pixels. You need to place it online in either the JPG or PNG format. It really doesn't matter which one you pick — whatever format your artwork comes in will be fine.

There are a number of simple ways to create album art. One of the easiest is the web application Canva (http://h2plink.com/Canva). The program has templates that you can quickly customize to your needs.

Another option is to get your album art custom designed. How much does this cost? Well, obviously, you can pay as much as you want, but a little-known site called Fiverr (http://h2plink.com/Fiverr — note the two R's) offers a marketplace of people who will do things for just five dollars. Truth be told, I've had most of my podcast album art created with one of their vendors. I love the world economy!

Finally, the question: "Can I make my own album art?" Yes, of course you can. But iTunes is filled with podcasts that no one takes seriously, because their album art screams "LOOK, SOMEONE WITH NO REAL GRAPHICS SKILLS MADE THIS!" If that's how you design (it's definitely how I design), stay away from making your own graphics. The old adage "you never get a second chance to make a first impression" is certainly relevant here, since your album art is the first introduction your audience gets to your podcast. Make sure it's a good one.

The Right Mindset

I hinted at this at the beginning of the chapter, but *please* — don't spend too much time on this. For 99% of you, your podcast host will write your feed, and for the rest of you, there are ridiculously easy ways to get it written for you.

The Feedburner Option (?)

In previous editions of this book I wrote about a service called Feedburner. In short, I no longer recommend this service, because the benefits it provides are no longer worth the effort.

If you don't know what Feedburner is, don't worry — it just isn't needed anymore.

A good host (such as Libsyn) offers you the chance to host your feed on your own domain name. That is an incredible insurance policy in case anything goes wrong.

If your host doesn't offer that option, find a host that does.

How Do I Know If my Feed is Working?

Since iTunes is the 800-pound gorilla of podcasting, most of you reading this book will have a copy installed on your computer. For the few of you who don't, install a copy now. You are going to need it to test and submit your feed to iTunes. I'll show you how to do this in the next chapter.

On occasion, I meet people who don't want to install iTunes on their computer for one reason or another. My advice: get over it. If you are going to play in a field where iTunes is the big player, you have to make sure your stuff work with iTunes.

Now that we got that over with, you can test your feed to see if it is working in iTunes by selecting the "Subscribe to Podcast" option and cutting and pasting your feed into the box iTunes provides. If it works in iTunes, then your feed is fully functional.

I've made a quick video of the process at http://h2plink.com/iTunesCheck. If iTunes changes the wording or the process, I'll make sure to update the video at that link.

Do I Need a Feed Validator?

If you've done any research in the podcasting space, you might have read about feed validators. These are programs that check your feed to make sure that there is nothing wrong with it. The most diligent of podcasters and tech-types will insist that you run your feed through a feed validator to make sure that all is well before you unleash your podcast on the public.

I've received emails from people telling me that my feed is "not validated" and has errors. In my opinion, the feed doesn't need to be validated, and I'm a little concerned about people who enjoy testing the feeds of others and reporting their findings — but that's another story altogether.

In my experience (gained from downloading millions of podcast episodes), a feed validator is simply overkill. A feed validator makes sure the feed is perfect for another computer — when all you really need to do is to make sure that when Frank from Idaho is looking for your podcast, he can find it.

With that said and done, if you are one of those check-everything-before-you-go-live types, there is no harm in running your feed through a validator — so have at it.

As I write this, I realize that by the time you finish reading there will probably be someone giving me a one-star review on Amazon, simply because of this section. Who knows, it might be you. If it isn't you and you've found the review I write of, nothing would do my heart more good than a response written by someone whose podcast is live and running because this book taught them how to focus on the stuff that really matters.

There It Is....

So, your media has been created and your feed is live. Now we need to tell a few people (especially iTunes) about it, so that you can start building the audience that you deserve. On to the next chapter!

Step 4 - Tell the World

First off — and I need to say this right out — this is NOT a book about marketing your podcast. This book is simply, as promised in the title, a book on "How To Podcast." Telling the world is part of that process.

This chapter is ONLY about getting the word out about your podcast in general so that, in short, when people are looking for you, they can find you. You'll probably want to do more than is explained in this book — however, in these next few pages I will give you everything you need to tell the world that your podcast exists. From there, go nuts with your promotion!

When you register this book (http://HowToPodcastBook.com/Register), I'll make sure to send you some additional content about marketing your show that expands on the concepts mentioned here.

With that said and done, let's get to work on telling the world.

Telling the World, in Short (and Tell Them to Subscribe While You're At It)

Telling the world about your podcast really comes down to two different steps: telling the directories that your show exists, and telling your own audience that you have a podcast they should be listening to.

By the way, don't just tell your audience that you have a podcast — tell them to *subscribe* to your podcast so that they can be informed every time you release a new episode. If you don't tell them to subscribe to the podcast, who will?

And of course, once you've made fans, tell them to spread the word about your show.

What Happens When I Release a New Episode?

Part of the beauty of podcasting is that it is a set-it-and-forget-it kind of thing. When you release a new episode, you don't need to do a single thing for others to receive it. The RSS feed you set up in the previous chapter automatically gets updated in the process of publishing, and the podcatching clients (such as iTunes) check on a regular basis and download or alert your audience as soon as they find something new. You don't have to do a thing.

I can't stress enough how cool this is. Whenever I release an episode of any of my podcasts, I've got people downloading it before I'm done finishing up the process — and as you see here, it's not a complicated process to close out. Literally within minutes of uploading my podcast to my host, I've got people all around the world downloading the thing.

The mechanics are all there — now I just need an audience to take advantage of them.

iTunes

iTunes is Apple's podcast directory. Different people with different agendas will tell you different numbers in terms of how many podcasts are downloaded through the iTunes directory (I've heard ranges from 60% to 95%), but there are two facts about this that are important to remember and will keep you focused.

Firstly, iTunes is *the* standard directory and will bring you many more times the amount of traffic than all the other directories combined. Get in that directory before you do anything else.

Secondly, iTunes is one of the easiest directories to submit your podcast to. It is a two minute process maximum, and here is a great video that will walk you through the procedure:

http://h2plink.com/SubmitToItunes

So, first things first: submit your podcast to iTunes, ONCE, and enjoy the benefits that come from it. Lately, Apple has been indexing podcasts submitted to iTunes in just a few days.

The Other Directories and Players

iTunes is not the only game in town, but it is the powerhouse of the podcasting industry. A number of other podcast clients grab their database content from iTunes (some legitimately, and some not so much), so just submitting there will get you almost everywhere you need to be.

There are a few other players in the podcast directory space that you'll want to pay attention to. However, I'm not going to list everybody with a directory because, quite simply, being listed in every available directory doesn't really matter.

Note: if you register this book, as I encouraged you to do at the beginning (http://www.HowToPodcastBook.com/Register), and a new important podcast directory arises, I'll be sure to let you know.

Stitcher

The most fascinating podcast play outside of iTunes is, in my opinion, Stitcher. Their integration into millions of car stereo systems, and their position as one of the top choices for Android users (tablet and otherwise), makes them a directory that your show needs to be on. The following link will explain how to get your podcast listed in Stitcher:

http://h2plink.com/GetOnStitcher

TuneIn

At the time of writing, the market penetration of TuneIn is not that exciting at all. I only see (as do most of my peers) a tiny percentage of listeners coming from TuneIn. They are worth mentioning because of their positioning in car stereo systems, and because this is the only "big name" that supports Windows phones. The number of users I see coming from TuneIn across any of the podcasts I have the stats for are, honestly, less than 1%. But Microsoft is upping their game, and the submission process is easy.

http://h2plink.com/GetOnTuneIn

I do have to mention that, at the time of writing, the Tesla electric car currently uses TuneIn as their podcasting client of choice. Again, I don't see any real numbers coming from

TuneIn, but I do like the idea that, should Elon Musk want to listen to me, I've made it possible.

iHeartRadio

In episode number ten of my show The Podcast Report (http://h2plink.com/TPR10), I interviewed Dave Jackson from The School Of Podcasting (http://h2plink.com/SOP) about how he got his show into iHeartRadio. I followed his direction and got The Podcast Report into iHeartRadio as well (http://h2plink.com/TPRIHR) — so the process works. If you want your show on iHeartRadio, listen to that episode. There are a few steps in the process, but I think it's worth it.

Some of you reading this will be surprised that iHeartRadio supports podcasts, while others will wonder why in the world you'd want your new media podcast listed in such an outdated directory. In short, listen to the interview with Dave for all of the reasons. But you should realize that iHeartRadio has spent millions advertising the platform — and you, my friend, can be found there as well.

I often joke from the stage that my Mom still believes that she can't listen to my shows because she doesn't own an iPod....but she *does* have iHeartRadio installed on her Android tablet.

SoundCloud

A number of podcasters have their show on SoundCloud (http://h2plink.com/SoundCloud). My research has shown that this option brings a minimal amount of listens, but it is still worth a paragraph or two here. SoundCloud is very interactive and very popular right now, and you might want to have your podcast associated with that brand. In addition, SoundCloud has a podcast hosting service. However, at this point, I can't recommend it.

The first thing that needs to be understood about SoundCloud is that it is not a directory. It is (at least at the time of this writing) a separate service, sort of like a YouTube of audio. Simply said, if you don't use them as your podcast host (and I STRONGLY recommend that you don't), you'll need to upload your audio podcasts to SoundCloud every time you publish an episode to your podcast host.

They do have a free option, but anyone with any significant body of work will probably need to pay for a premium account to host their podcast at SoundCloud.

If you are carefully tracking your podcast downloads, remember that because SoundCloud pulls from their own library, you'll want to add your SoundCloud stats to whatever tracking you are doing.

To be honest, I don't currently host any of my shows at SoundCloud. However, I do have clients who are there and are seeing some interesting interactions on the site.

Google Play

New to the Podcast directory world in 2016, finally, is Google. At the time this was written, the directory was not yet active (nor was impact determined), but Google has promised a release "soon" and you are able to submit your Podcast right now. I certainly recommend doing so (and will update this part of the book once something more is known).

h2plink.com/SubmitToGoogle

Google Play is, for lack of a better description, "The iTunes For Google Devices." Almost anyone with an Android device has access to the store and Google is expected to push it even more once the Podcast Directory is released.

What will the impact of Podcasts in Google Play be? It is important to note, that although Google holds the highest percentage of "smart" devices, the significant numbers are largely from low-end devices, not typically associated with media consumption. As of I now, I doubt the Google Play directory will have any significant impact on the industry, but the size of Google's impact and the massive amounts of Android devices dictate that I put it here.

It is also important to note that although the Kindle Fire devices from Amazon are, technically, Android devices, they have a different "store," managed by Amazon. At this point, no Amazon Podcast Directory (or Client) has been announced.

Google Search

You don't just want to have your podcast in the directories. You want to make sure Google and the other directories know that your podcast exists, so that when someone enters your name or topic into the search engines, the website for your podcast shows up. It's just common sense.

The great thing about Google is that you really don't have to do anything anymore to let Google know that you exist. Once some other site somewhere links to you, Google will find you and index your site as well. Just linking to your site when you submit your podcast to iTunes will do the trick.

If you want a quick way to get Google to index your podcast website, write a post in Google+ which links to your site — Google will do the rest.

What About Directory "X" That You Didn't List?

There are hundreds of podcast directories. In my opinion (and hey, it's my book), once you pass the ones listed here, you simply don't get the return on your time to make it worthwhile.

With that in mind, if you still want a master list, Rob Walch from Libsyn and the Podcast 411 show keeps a fairly up-to-date list at http://h2plink.com/RobsDirectory. Also popular is Daniel J. Lewis's "Podcast Places" (http://h2plink.com/PodcastPlaces).

The Dirty Little Secret About Podcast Directories

As cool as podcast directories are, they are for a very specific audience: people who like podcasts and want to know if there are additional shows that match their interests. This is a very small segment of the world, making directories a lousy place to put all your focus when building an audience.

You are not going to build any real audience just by being in a podcast directory — or all of them — even if you are uniquely positioned inside.

This might surprise you, but when Apple listed my show The Podcast Report (http://h2plink.com/ThePodcastReport) in a special "How To Podcast" section in iTunes, *it made no measurable difference to my audience size.* Think about it — what better promotion could my podcast get from them? I asked a few other podcasters on the list if they saw anything different and the answer was always "no." Does this mean iTunes is worthless? No. It just means that the iTunes audience is a small segment of the podcasting world, and not the only source for someone to build their audience. In short, podcast directories are a small piece of the podcast promotion process.

Where Do Listeners Come From?

When Kevin Costner released that silly *Field Of Dreams* movie, I honestly think he did a lot more damage than good. Too many people now believe that "if you build it, they will come" (in other words, if they launch their podcast, people will simply find them and listen/subscribe). Nothing could be further from the truth. I've met too many people who simply don't understand why, now that their podcast is out, they don't have the listening audience of Howard Stern or Rush Limbaugh.

Sigh....

I'm going to be honest: the submission process I've listed here won't bring that much of an audience at all. It's better than nothing, sure. But it is your duty and your job to get the word out about your podcast. The rest of this chapter contains a few thoughts on that process.

Start Building Your Audience with the Audience You Already Have

Let's start building a podcast audience with the people who already know, like and trust you. There is no better place to start a podcast audience than with them.

You'd be surprised how many times I've had someone with a massive audience on another media ask me how to get the word out about their podcast. No matter how big or small your existing audience is, you need to tell them that you have a podcast and that they should check it out. Think about it — how else are they going to find out? It's not like they regularly log into iTunes and search to see if you are there.

In addition to telling them that you have a podcast, let them know: a) how to listen, and b) how to subscribe. When you tell them how to subscribe, make sure they know the benefits they get for doing so. If you don't know yourself, take a few minutes to figure that out.

How do you do this? Any way possible. Email is best if you already have an email list.

However you currently communicate with your audience is the best way for you to tell them about your podcast. If you do voicemail or SMS blasts, send one out about your podcast. If you have a dry erase board at your place of business, make sure you write a message on it asking people to subscribe.

I have one client who doubled their audience when they added a paper insert about their podcast to their monthly billing envelopes.

How can YOU best reach your audience with information about your show?

Enlisting Your Audience to Spread the Word

Once the people who know, like and trust you are listening to your podcast, you need to *ask them to share your show with others*. Give them a reason and the means to do so. This might seem odd to you at first, but you must realize that it will never happen if you don't ask.

This will result in one of two things: either they will share your show with others (and what better evangelist for your show than someone who already likes you?), or they won't. If they won't, you need to ask yourself (and them) why. If your show isn't worth telling others about, you need to change your show!

Don't know how to make your show worth sharing? Ask your audience — the people who are already listening are often more than willing to share their thoughts with you. If they're listening, plugging you into their earbuds or taking you with them on their morning commute, you have an intimacy with your audience that means you can ask for such feedback.

Of course, don't put it all on them — make it easy to share your show. A Facebook page for your show is a great first step. You can see the one we've built for The Podcast Report at http://h2plink.com/TPRFacebook.

Cross-Promotion

Another excellent way to build a podcast audience is by reaching out to *existing podcasts already catering to your audience*. Initially this may seem counterintuitive, but it works. It never hurts to approach other shows in your sphere to see if they'd be interested in cross-promoting.

You'll find most podcasters to be some of the most sharing and helpful people you'll ever meet. Reach out to them and see if there is a chance for some cross-promotion — you might be surprised at what they come up with.

Here's a little secret trick of podcast cross-promotion, so that you can get some exposure without having to ask for too much: reach out to a show you want to be highlighted on, and see if you can interview the host. The chances are good that they'll say yes — and of course, once the episode is released, chances are they will want to share it with their audience.

What Separates Your Podcast From All the Others is What Will Grow Your Audience More than Anything Else

Here's a little exercise that can do amazing things for you. Complete the following sentence:

The thing that separates my podcast from all the others in my genre is _____.

Once you figure that out, you have a reason to promote, and a specific promotional element that separates you from everyone else.

One Last Promotion Opportunity

We've set up a Facebook page for this book at http://www.Facebook.com/HowToPodcast. When you publish your podcast, make sure to post it there — we'd all like to learn from you and be inspired by you. Hopefully, that might bring a little promotion to your show as well.

Tell the World

Hopefully I've started you along on the process of telling the world about your podcast. The podcast directories now know that you exist, so people looking for you there can find you. Google has you indexed, which is great for common searches. You have alerted your audience and have started doing what you can to build from there.

Great job!

Step 4 Completed: NOW WHAT?

My goal for this book was always to show you how to quickly and easily you can create a podcast. We've done that — but your journey has just begun.

Don't worry, the book doesn't stop here! Turn the page for more (or keep scrolling if you're doing the digital thing).

Your Bonuses / Register This Book

I can't tell you how thrilled I am to offer this bonus package to everyone who purchased this book. The thought that I could offer many times what you paid for this book in bonuses is a thrill and a half for me, and should hopefully make your purchase of this book a no-brainer.

My rule for all bonuses in this book is that they can't be imaginary bonuses with faked values just to bring up the final number. Everything on this list sells online, at the time of this writing, for the very price listed below. How cool is that?

Now with that said and done, I have to point out that **any of these deals can change at any time** - that's just the nature of the beast.

I will also tell you that I am working on more bonuses, but since they weren't official at the time this went to publication, I can't list them here.

To get access to all of these bonuses, I need you to register your book. You can do that here:

http://HowToPodcastBook.com/Register

Once we verify your email and purchase, I'll send you access directions for everything listed and any updates on additional offers I was able to get for you.

Your first bonus is a six-month subscription to *Podertainment Magazine*. This online magazine comes from the world of Gary

Leland, creator of the original Podcast Pickle directory and good friend. Issues run at $2.99 each - and for you, the first six of them are free. Register for more details.

Your next bonus is a membership at LegalPodcastMusic.com (everyone else pays $37). Looking for music to put into your podcast without any legal problems? Look no further. Register today.

Dave Jackson is willing to take $50 off your first month at The School of Podcasting if you register your book. Thanks Dave.

http://HowToPodcastBook.com/Register

I've arranged for my recommended podcast hosting platform Libsyn to give you your first month of hosting for free. Depending on what level you come in at, that's up to a $75 deal. Register today!

http://HowToPodcastBook.com/Register

Also, I do a yearly online training event called *How to Build a List With Your Podcast* that is currently selling online for $199. If you register before the event takes place, your ticket will be free. If you register afterwards, I'll make sure you get an online replay of the event.

In addition, when you register the book, I'll be able to keep you up to date with everything related to the book and pass along any news in the podcasting space that I think is important to you. This is one of those systems which allows you to unsubscribe at any time, so if you get bored of hearing from me, you're only one click away from silence.

With that said and done, what's stopping you?

http://HowToPodcastBook.com/Register

What's Next?

You now know how to podcast. You're also probably pretty surprised at how easy it is if you've made it this far in the book.

You have everything you need - and those great bonuses too (if you registered the book, *natch*)!

Honestly, nothing would thrill me more than to have you simply close this book, record your first podcast, get it live and post your success story on our Facebook page.

http://www.Facebook.com/HowToPodcast

Remember, as an attendee of the Genius Network Event, I'd be thrilled to set up a complimentary Podcast review session with you, details are here:

http://PaulColligan.com/GeniusNetwork

Thanks for coming along on this journey with me.

Obviously, the journey is about more than just creating a podcast and making it available to the world (although this first step is pretty critical ;-)). Once you are live, you need to use it to expand your reach to as many people as is possible and leverage the tech of this exciting platform to build your business.

Finally, in addition to everything included in these pages, I've got some additional content that didn't fit into this book which we would like to get to you. Make sure you register your book at http://www.HowToPodcastBook.com/Register to get it all.

Finally, at the time of writing, I'm more than 60 episodes into The Podcast Report over at http://ThePodcastReport.com. If you interested in more of the business of podcasting, do drop on by and subscribe to the show.

I close, asking a simple question:

When will you record your first episode?

Paul Colligan

Portland, Oregon

Expand Reach - Leverage Tech

PART 2 - HOW OTHERS PODCAST

How Others Podcast

Books are a tricky business. You save someone time and pages getting to the point directly, and although some will thank you, others will post a review on Amazon complaining about how short your book was.

We can't have that, can we?

I thought it would be fun to end this book with a few articles and interviews from some people I like, some people you may have heard of and a few people I bet you haven't heard of, in order to inspire you on your podcast journey.

You will notice that all of them are focused on getting great content out there and not on making things complicated. This is a lesson we can all learn from.

I start the series with interviews from John Lee Dumas and Michael Stelzner. John is a media making machine and Michael just launched his second podcast. There is a lot to learn from both of these guys - their podcasts are always at the top of their categories and have seen millions of downloads of their shows. If you don't know about them already, you should.

After that we have Amy Porterfield and Ed Rush - two great people that I've worked with on past projects who knock it out of the park with their podcasts. Notice Amy's ability to make the complex simple and watch how Ed only launches strategically.

We then have a batch of articles that I'm REALLY excited about:

I offered listeners of **The Podcast Report** the ability to share their take on my simple approach to podcasting. Listeners John Cote, Mary-Lynn Foster, Fred Castaneda, Steve Cardinal, Dave Bullis, and Tom Stewart all responded - and I include them in this book. Among this batch you've got long-timers and newbies sharing valuable real world tips and experience everyone can use.

I then close out this section with a batch of articles from a relatively new player in the space who is becoming more and more important to my process every day - Auphonic. Finally, I end with outstanding pieces by Dave Jackson, Gary Leland and Chris Christensen - three guys who have been part of the podcasting space pretty much since day one.

Again I want to stress that these additional chapters *are just the icing on the cake - you already have everything you need to get started in the previous chapters.* I include these supplemental chapters to give you a well-rounded approach to podcasting, something I believe we all need (and that these authors do perfectly).

By the way, I intend on doing an update to this book in 2016. Maybe your story can be included? Make sure you tell us about the podcast you launched as a result of this book at our Facebook page - http://www.Facebook.com/HowToPodcast. You might be surprised what can come from it.

John Lee Dumas on Making Media

*The following is a transcript from Episode #30 of **The Podcast Report** (http://h2plink.com/ThePodcastReport) where I interviewed John Lee Dumas of **Entrepreneur On Fire** (http://h2plink.com/EntrpreneurOnFire) about his strategies for Rapid Content Production. John is a MACHINE when it comes to content creation (he does a show every day of the week) and I want to have him spill the beans a bit about his methods. Take note of John's generous offerings in the bonus chapter.*

Paul Colligan:

> I'm on the Skype line with John Lee Dumas, **Entrepreneur on Fire**. Sir, you've said it so many times. *Are you ready to... ignite?*

John Lee Dumas:

> Paul, let's set this place on fire.

Paul Colligan:

> Let's do it my friend. I am impressed with what you've done and it's funny, because some of the things I'm impressed with are not the same things which others are impressed with. Maybe that means I've got bad focus... but hey, it's my show - so let's get to work here. The first thing is: you produce a considerable amount of content.
>
> I've been on your show. You sent me the questionnaire.

You ask the same questions to everybody. Everybody is familiar with the questions; they like the questions; they're familiar. How much additional time do you spend on your show producing content other than the interviews that you do?

John Lee Dumas:

Not much, is the answer. What we have set up is really a system that does flow just like you shared. We have our studio days, which are just Tuesdays with eight back-to-back interviews. By 6 p.m. that night, I not only have interviewed eight people, but it is edited, it is produced and it is (for the most part) uploaded and ready to go on that one day. From that point, it's all my virtual assistants; they take over. They're the ones who set up the processes, the follow-ups, the marketing of it in the social media which keeps the machine going. It really was a system that I set up at a large cost and with a lot of time - once. Now it just works for me.

Paul Colligan:

A 40-minute show takes you 40 minutes to make?

John Lee Dumas:

I'd say a 40-minute show takes me 50 minutes to make. That's because I do drop markers throughout the interviews; for example, if there's a swear word or something a little excessive. I might go in and splice that out - but it's super minimal. I'd say I spend no more than 5-10 minutes on that per show.

Paul Colligan:

Awesome. This is something which I think gets missed. Now, you mentioned the batching and a lot of people know about it, but there are like three people left on the planet who still don't know about you, my friend. You said that you tape all of your shows on Tuesday, did I hear that right? This is obviously a leading question: you do eight interviews on Tuesday?

John Lee Dumas:

Yes. First off, I hope those three people who have not heard about me are listening to you, Paul. Starting at 9 a.m. every Tuesday, I do an interview on the hour, every single hour, until 4 p.m. That's when my last interview starts. By the time 5 p.m. rolls around, I have eight interviews complete. By the time 6 p.m. hits, I've edited those at an average rate of five minutes a clip for all eight - and I'm done for that week, plus one day of interviews. As we sit here right now, I'm actually booked out every single Tuesday for the next three-and-a-half months. I know that Tuesday is a full studio day.

Paul Colligan:

That's one day, and I won't say one fifth of your week because I know you work like a mad man, but...

John Lee Dumas:

One seventh.

Paul Colligan:

One eight-hour session and all the shows are done.

John Lee Dumas:

Done.

Paul Colligan:

Does that exhaust you? How do you have the energy to do that? Talk to me.

John Lee Dumas:

I do equate it a little bit to training for a marathon. I'm not a great runner. I do jog every now and then but after two miles I'm done, put a fork in me... and that's pretty much it. However, I have trained for half marathons and marathons before and I could never run either one of those right now - but I could train and then eventually be able to run one.

When I first started *Entrepreneur on Fire*, Paul, I was

71

doing three or four interviews a day, two or three days a week. I was toast at the end of those days. I saw how much time it took me to set up for each one, then to break down for each one. It was becoming my week. So, that's when I decided to draw a line in the sand and say, "It's got to be one day and basically, I've got to build up the energy for this." Just like you can build up running energy, I wanted to build up interviewing energy. It hasn't come easy. It's definitely been a process, and with every single month that has gone by, it has become a little bit easier. But there were times that at the end, I felt near to collapsing or saying, "Okay, I need some spaghetti. I need a blanket. That's it - no more." Now, honestly, I can do eight interviews and be like, "Alright, what's next? Let's do a live webinar." It's gotten to that point; but it did take a while and it was a process to get here.

Paul Colligan:

Would it be easier to do two sets of four interviews, take two half days or something like that?

John Lee Dumas:

I think it would have been when I started. That's probably where I should have stayed longer to be honest, because it would have resulted in higher quality interviews. Back in the 300s and 400s of my interview episodes, back when it really still was a strain for me, by episode six, seven and eight, I was flagging mentally. It was just kind of hard to conjure up that same type of energy. It's pretty funny; I just interviewed somebody for episode 872. I also interviewed her for episode 61. I went back and just listened to a couple of minutes of that first interview right before I kicked into our second interview. I was like, "Wow!" I was uninspiring; I was so flat. I had no energy in that interview compared to what I have now. That came with feeling more comfortable and doing it more often; also, she was probably episode seven or eight of the day on the first interview, and I was just flagging at that point.

But to be honest with you, now, I look forward to each interview of the eight. I get really fired up just getting into these conversations. I'm at the point where I love my eight-interview days. Firstly, because I can do it without breaking sweat. Secondly, because it doesn't take up blocks of my other days where I'm doing other things: creating courses, writing books, doing all the cool things that need to be done.

Paul Colligan:

That's good. That's good. Now, again, for those three people who haven't heard of you, every episode of your show follows a format. You send the interviewee a batch of questions. You ask the questions and you do it. It's brilliant, because it makes it easier for you and you don't have to do a tremendous amount of research. I was listening to an interview with Tony Robbins and he said he does 18 hours of research before he meets with somebody. I was like, "Oh my goodness." You don't have to do any research and you could probably do all the questions by heart now. I imagine that for your first 500 shows, you had a cheat sheet. After that, it's probably just second nature to you.

What I found interesting is that there are a lot of podcasters, unfortunately, who have decided that if they just have a batch of questions and if they just do eight a week, they'll see the same success that you've had. It's a bad concept and it's a bad idea; largely just because this is is the formula that works for you. This is the model that works for you. This is what makes your nature happen. It wasn't that you stumbled across this. You did a heck of a lot of work, a heck of a lot planning, a heck of a lot of strategy before all this happened and said, "Hey, this is a formula that makes sense to John." What would you say to somebody who's trying to create content, trying to come up with a formula that makes sense to Fred or to Becky or to Frank?

John Lee Dumas:

I love the question - and before I answer, I just want to go back and reiterate how correct you are on the initial point that you made, which is that when I wake up on Tuesday morning, I don't even know who the eight people are that I'm going to be interviewing. That's because I haven't yet opened up my spreadsheet that my VA creates and she updates. It's literally sometimes only ten minutes before my interview starts when I'll pull it up and say, "Okay here's my eight people. Oh, I know. I know that person and that person a little bit. I've heard of that person." I don't have to know who I'm going to be interviewing, because of the system I've set up; it doesn't require me to know anything before the interview starts, because I have those formatted questions.

In a way, I like not knowing too much because it makes me curious and it makes me, in my opinion, ask the questions to follow up their answers that I would want, that I hope and want my listeners on Fire Nation to be asking. That's just kind of a little reiteration on a point that you made that I definitely want to second. It's huge for me because it just takes away so much mental bandwidth - like what you mentioned with Tony Robbins. I can't do 18 hours of prep! I don't even take 18 minutes for eight interviews to prep, I don't. It's just all right there. All I know is their 50-word intro that I'm reading over once right before I introduce them, when I usually have them on Skype already.

To answer your last question, for someone who's listening right now and they're saying, "I want to create something, but how do I know what the right frequency is? How do I know what the right content is? How do I know this, how do I know that?" I created

Entrepreneur on Fire because it was what I wanted. I was so tired of listening to a great podcast episode with an inspiring entrepreneur, getting so much out of it and then knowing that I have to wait two more weeks, or another week for that next interview. I also hated those interviews where people were going on and on about cats, or maybe they're talking about sports one day, but they weren't quite getting to the meat. I thought, "To me, the perfect podcast would be seven days a week." I knew that if I press the play button, I was going to hear what I wanted to hear. That I was going to hear an actual journey from a successful entrepreneur who is going to be sharing their failures, their lessons learned, their "Aha!" moments, their success.

I thought, "I want that. I want to give that to Fire Nation." Boom - *Entrepreneur on Fire* was born. That was how my show came about. If you're listening right now, that's how your show needs to come about. You need to really get angry or frustrated or depressed because the show you want to listen to doesn't exist. When you know what that show is, then you go out and give birth to it and create it. That's going to ensure that you're drawing people in and that the audience is going to resonate with you as a host and your content as a whole.

Paul Colligan:

There are two things I love about you, John... well, there

are a lot, but we're just going to list two for now. Firstly, you have a crystal clear understanding of who your avatar is. You've said that from day one, "I am the avatar. I'm making the show the I want to listen to." Now, not everybody has that opportunity, not everybody has that gift, for lack of a better term, but you're crystal clear about it. That's what anybody can take away from this.

Secondly, the thing that I really love is that the secret to your success - one of the many secrets to your success - is not the formula. It's not the excitement. It's not the "fire" part of it. It is the fact that you have such a close and intimate relationship with your avatar. You know exactly who you're creating for. There is no doubt why your podcast is and what your podcast is in your mind.

That clarity is phenomenal. That clarity is worth a million bucks. What would you say to people struggling to figure out their avatar? Or spending too much time on content creation and editing because they're not quite sure what they want? Maybe we don't have the intimacy that John has with his avatar, but how can we get that kind of intimacy?

John Lee Dumas:

Avatar is everything, in my opinion, when it comes to creating a podcast. I think one thing that a lot of people do miss is that they think about what their avatar has to be in some way, in broad shapes and forms. I say that because every time I speak in a conference or I'm talking and I get asked this question on someone else's podcast, then I always turn the question around and I say, "Who out there has a podcast? Okay raise your hand. Okay, how long have you been podcasting? Oh, you have 100 episodes a year. You must know who your one perfect listener is, who that avatar is. Stand up and share with the world."

Sure enough, they'll puff their chest out and they'll stand up and they'll say, "My avatar is males between ages 25 and 45 who like to drink coffee and watch football on the weekends." I'm like, that's barely a targeted demographic. That is not an avatar; you don't know who your avatar is. I've given my avatar spiel a lot. My avatar is Jimmy. He is identical to who I was when I launched *Entrepreneur on Fire.*

I know exactly who that person is. Whenever I come to a fork in the road, I don't make that decision; it's not my bandwidth, it's Jimmy's bandwidth, because he knows, left or right, straight off the bat. If you're listening right now, you're saying, "I'm struggling to create my avatar because I want so many people to listen. I want to grow a large audience." Remember, if you try to resonate with everybody and make a vague avatar to resonate with everybody, you're going to resonate with nobody. You need to be one of these people who says, "You know what, I know exactly one person who would be perfect to listen to my podcast, and I'm going to create my podcast for that person." Get a niche in there.

Actually, just get a handhold and start building a little momentum. Then start having that momentum work outwards. You can expand the scope outwards from that point and grow a bigger show; you can go from niching down to bringing it back out. Just go out and grow a bigger audience. But so many of us, Paul, are afraid to start small. Because we think if we start small, we'll always be small. But the problem is, we have to start small to get big. If we start big, we'll never even get going because we'll just get lost in this ocean. I've seen it time and time again. There's over 1,900 people in **Podcaster's Paradise**. I watch their launches and I watch their trajectory.

Those that are still crushing it six, twelve or eighteen months later, are those that just say, "You know what? This is the perfect listener. I'm going to podcast to that person until I've dominated that niche. Then I'm going to take one step back out. Then I'm going to build this larger audience as I continue to move outwards." Those are the people who have found success. Don't be afraid to get specific, to start really focused in and just be that avatar if it's you, or create that avatar if it's somebody else.

Paul Colligan:

Who do you think is doing this, and you probably know a lot of them, especially with 1,900 right now in **Podcaster's Paradise** (http://h2plink.com/Paradise), you said?

John Lee Dumas:

Yes.

Paul Colligan:

You probably know a lot of them. Pick someone that maybe we'd have a better chance than others to recognize. Who else out there do you think really understands their avatar?

John Lee Dumas:

I would actually just like to poll up our Facebook group, because it's so cool to see these discussions and these hangouts that we do and how focused the actual word "avatar" is in my community (**Paradise** - (http://h2plink.com/Paradise). To see these people going back and forth, saying, "That's not niche enough. That's not focused enough." But one person who I love talking about is Paul Blaise. He has a podcast called *Potters Cast*. It's about making pots. It's handcrafted pots.

Picture the movie *Ghost*, Paul. Paul Blaise is like that; it's a podcast for people who actually make pots like in the movie *Ghost*; handcrafted pots. His podcast is so specific, so focused. If he gets 600 listens per episode, it's a good day. In fact, it's a great day, because 600 people who are listening to a podcast about how to make pottery, hand-thrown pottery, is a massive audience for that niche. He knows that exact avatar. He knows the age of that person. He knows where that person is going; he knows they are going to their local college at night to take the courses.

He knows how he can reach out to colleges and have them mention his podcast during their courses. He brings in those teachers, who actually teach these college communication courses at these state universities and community colleges around the country, onto his show. They share it with their students... and then it starts to spread like wildfire within the community. That's an example of a guy who does a podcast about making pots. He's having a great time doing it, because it's his passion and he's very successful with it.

Paul Colligan:

Beautiful. I will get that in the show notes and in the transcript. We'll get a link for that to happen as well. I'm going to want to close this up, but I'm going to be respectful of your time. Do you have any final words? Part one of the book is "Make Digital Media". That's the first step, and you just started making media like a racehorse out the traps. I love that, because I've met people (and I'm sure I said that you probably met them too) who six months later have yet to hit the record button. What would you say to someone who's just a deer in the headlights when it comes to making media, and has yet to hit that red button? What would you say to them, John?

John Lee Dumas:

Paul, I love this. I love to make media. One of my favorite quotes, which ties right in with this and really just underscores this and helped me to get this far, is: "If you want to be, do." I wanted to be a podcaster, Paul. I had zero experience; I had zero online presence; I'd never spoken into a microphone before or interviewed anybody... but I wanted to be a podcaster. The only way that I was going to be a podcaster was by doing that thing, was by podcasting.

I was willing to have the courage to be bad, because it does take that courage. For a decent amount of time, slowly getting better by practicing the craft, by pressing that red button every single day, talking to somebody that was so much more successful, so much more eloquent, so much more polished, so much more impressive than me; bumbling around, acting the fool, stumbling over my words, trying to have a coherent conversation.

But every time I'd think: "Wow, that was bad, but I did

a little bit better on this or on that." I'm just doing that every single day and now I'm at episode 835. That is the reality of just doing; that's why I love making media. I would ask them, "What are you doing? I don't want to hear any excuses. You're about to say 10 reasons why you're not making media? Make media." That's all that matters and that's why I love that message.

Paul Colligan:

Do we have an attribution for "If you want to be, do," or does that come from you?

John Lee Dumas:

I've Googled it over and over; I've looked everywhere. Brainy Quotes seems to have everything, but right now I just can't find out who to attribute that quote to. I'm tempted to take it... but I know that I've heard it from somewhere else.

Paul Colligan:

Very cool John. Thank you so much, man. It's about making media. You do it with an enthusiasm and, dare I say, a fire that I see nobody else doing it with. You do it with a great amount of strategy and understanding and empathy towards your avatar, which gets the results. It's a great formula, I'm glad you're doing it, I love the

83

show. But it's your understanding of what you are doing which produced this formula, and I think that is such a testimony to what you've got there. Thank you so much for the interview, man. I want to be good to your time. Thanks.

John Lee Dumas:

Paul, with those words, I can die happy, my friend. Thank you kindly.

Paul Colligan:

There it is, John in all his glory. I love this guy. I love what he's doing, I love what he's done, I love the model that he's created. I'm thrilled to share him with you, *The Podcast Report* audience.

You Don't Need a Microphone to Make a Podcast (With Michael Stelzner)

I said in Part One that you don't always need a microphone to do your podcast and this interview shows you a great example of how true that statement is. I got to hear about Michael Stelzner's new podcast (less than a month old at the time of this interview) a few weeks before everyone else did and knew it was going to be something special. Michael always does things right and there is something for everyone to learn from this interview.

Paul Colligan:

> I am on the Skype line with Michael Stelzner of Social Media Examiner. Michael and I met a long time ago at an event in San Diego in... what hotel was it, Mike? It was a Holiday Inn or something?

Michael Stelzner:

> That's right, man. That was before I'd even launched Social Media Examiner. I can't remember; somewhere in a hotel circle, but you blew me away back then and I knew nothing about social media. That was probably 2008; late 2008.

Paul Colligan:

> The video from that event still gets played on YouTube a lot and it's funny because it's 4:3, it's not 16:9. That's how long ago this was. It feels like the old days. Mike

has just... everybody knows him from Social Media Examiner, which is a runaway hit on a lot of levels and is exciting to watch. As a friend, it's exciting just to see Mike's success. It's a blast, but then again at the same time, I know whenever Mike does something, he's going to do it with not just the enthusiasm it deserves and not just the gravitas it deserves but he'll spend the money he needs to spend. He'll spend the time he needs to spend. He won't launch until it's done and these are things that I really, really admire about the guy. What Mike did was, Mike launched a second podcast. Now, podcast number one, the Social Media Examiner show... what's the right name for that?

Michael Stelzner:

The original show that's been around for about two-and-a-half years is called the *Social Media Marketing Podcast* (http://hp2link.com/SMMPodcast).

Paul Colligan:

That's right. The *Social Media Marketing Podcast.* It comes out once a week, it's a blast, good stuff. You keep up with the jungle theme. I don't know what the numbers are and you don't even necessarily need to share them, but any look at iTunes will tell you that Mike is doing quite well with this show.

I remember at last year's Social Media Marketing World

event at the keynote (it wasn't by any means a scientific experiment, but) you asked the audience to raise their hand if they listened to the show and it was about one third, if I remember it right?

Michael Stelzner:

Absolutely, yeah. We found that a lot of people feed at the well, if you will, of our weekly show and they are the most faithful, loyal fans that we have and yeah, about 30% of the people that attend most of our events are weekly listeners to our show. For us, that's a huge benefit of a podcast.

Paul Colligan:

Not satisfied with that, the other thing I love about Mike is his hunger. You launched a daily show, but in just realizing the realities of the space-time continuum and the fact that you want to see your kids, this one is not voiced by Mike.

This is not you doing a daily show. You brought somebody else out. Tell me what's this new show? Why did you launch it and what's it like doing a podcast without ever talking into a microphone?

Michael Stelzner:

This is actually our third show, Paul. I don't know if you remember but I did launch a show called *Parenting*

Adventures and we did 12 episodes of that. Running those two shows back-to-back was really challenging, because I was doing the interviews on both of those shows and they were for very different audiences.

We called a day on that project in the fall of last year but this time around, here was the thought, Paul: we have millions of people who are reading the Social Media Examiner and we put out articles that are pretty detailed.

They tend to be 1,500 words or longer and one of the things that we started to see with some of the smaller blogs in the space was that they were getting some of their content and they were translating it into audio. When I say smaller blogs, these are people who are thought to be leaders, who have their own blog and who use their own voice.

I thought to myself, "Man, you know, we're sitting on a goldmine of content here. I wonder if we could select some of the best content and abridge it (if you will), and create a show without telling anyone what we're really doing, but create a show that is a daily 10-minute show."

We call this show the snack; the *Social Media Examiner Show* (http://h2plink.com/SMEPcast) is the snack and the *Social Media Marketing Podcast* is the meal, right? Because it's a 45-minute weekly show, whereas the Social Media Examiner show is a 10-

minute show. As of this recording, we're only about two-and-a-half weeks into this project.

Paul Colligan:

Now, you are not the voice. Who is the voice? Where did you get the voice?

Michael Stelzner:

I am not the voice for a couple of reasons; first of all, as you mentioned, I am not very scalable. Secondly, we hire professional voice talent, so we put out the word and a lot of people applied. Frankly, it's very hard to read something and not sound like you're reading.

We found this gal named Chelsea, and I purposely don't put her last name on there because I am not trying to establish Chelsea as a thought leader. She is nothing more than a voice. She is nothing more than a verbal conduit for our content.

She does a great job because she does not sound like she's reading. I can talk a little bit about this Paul, if you want to, but to get our articles ready for her is a pretty significant undertaking.

Paul Colligan:

Yeah please, let's chat about that; but first, I just want to make sure everybody gets this and understands the concept - because what we've got here is a show which comes out every weekday, comprised entirely of existing content from the archives read by somebody else.

One of the things I love is your editorial process; your crap-detector and -eliminator which makes sure that the stuff which comes out is good. What do you go through to get content that Chelsea can read which makes it sound like it's not being read?

Michael Stelzner:

First, let me tell you what we are striving towards. Currently we are publishing four days a week. We're striving towards five days a week and what we are trying to do is we are trying to get the process down to be really, really fast - and what I mean by that is, we would love to have the audio for the articles of this week that are published on Social Media Examiner. Right now, it's just too early for us to be able to get to that point. We would even love to have last week's articles available on audio for this week, if you follow where I am going with that.

Paul Colligan:

Yeah.

Michael Stelzner:

What we do currently is we have a lot of data (as anyone does who has Google Analytics on their website), so we can look at the articles from the past few weeks and we can see which articles tend to perform very well for us on the metrics that we care about.

Those tend to be traffic to the site, social shares and email conversions. We look at the ones that convert really well for us and then what we do, Paul, is we say, "Okay, will this translate into audio?" An article on Google Analytics is probably not going to translate into audio because you've got to show a lot of screen shots, right, and you've got to explain things with visuals.

What we've decided to do is pick the articles which work really well in audio. Then what we do is we have one of our editors who literally goes in and scrubs the article to prepare it for audio. She removes content which will not translate into audio.

She puts in verbal cues in there, like, "Hey at the end of this show we're going to mention a link." If there is a screenshot of a Heinz Ketchup campaign, she translates what's happening in the picture into verbals.

A great example is Heinz Ketchup; on the podcast, we'll talk briefly about how they used Instagram and what they did, whereas we would never say that in the article because it shows it with a visual. Essentially, it's like an audiobook. An abridged audiobook.

Paul Colligan:

There are your two best practices, right away. Best practice number one: you actually tracked what you were doing and you figured out which articles people were interested in, what your audience wanted (for lack of a better term) more of. That's the stuff that you picked to do.

Then you recognized the medium difference, and that what worked great in an article is going to need a couple of adjustments to work in audio.

Michael Stelzner:

Exactly. It's more than just a couple, it's a lot. That's absolutely true and surprisingly, it works really well; and then we give the voice talent some freedom. Because there are things that the editor who does the preparing of the article for the voice, there are things that she can't think about because she's not the voice talent.We allow the voice talent a little bit of creative freedom to alter the script, as long as she doesn't change the intent of the message.

Paul Colligan:

Very cool, very cool. That probably gives her a little bit more freedom. It's not just a gig, she begins to show her personality, she begins to bring a little bit of herself into it.

Michael Stelzner:

We also chose two voices. We've got a male voice who does the opening introduction to the show, who mentions the name of the show and then the female voice is the one who does the show. We purposely chose younger voices.

I am 46 and we wanted to appeal to a younger audience, because we also knew that a lot of the next generation of podcast listeners are young, hip 20- and 30-somethings, mostly in the 20-something range. They don't have a lot of time, so the goal of keeping this thing to 10 minutes for them is extremely palatable.

We're getting messages from a lot of people saying, "I'm listening when I'm in line at the checkout," or "It's perfect for when I take my kids to school." It's been really, really cool. I was surprised and frankly a little scared that it might cannibalize my other show.

Paul Colligan:

Let's chat about that. Has it? Have you seen any decline in the other show?

Michael Stelzner:

We've seen zero decline. We've actually seen an increase, surprisingly. We have actually seen a dramatic increase in the downloads of the other show this month. We cannot say for certain why that is, other than maybe just the fact that we've been evangelizing our podcast and maybe some people are discovering both of them in the same swoop... but it's actually gone up, surprisingly.

Paul Colligan:

Are you cross-marketing the two shows between each other?

Michael Stelzner:

We're not cross-marketing the original, longer show from the new show. We are only cross-marketing the bigger audience; the *Social Media Marketing Podcast* does promote the smaller show, but we've only done it once.

What we did was we came out with a special episode. We normally publish on a Friday, but this time we came out with a special Saturday episode where I introduced the new show, said who it was for and then literally took the first episode and put it in the other show. Do you understand where I'm going with that?

Paul Colligan:

Yeah, yeah.

Michael Stelzner:

> Then I said at the end of the show, "If you want to subscribe to this show, here's where to find it." We were expecting to see declines (as you always do when you do a launch) but in reality, it's been extremely steady.
>
> It's been pretty impressive. Now, I must admit that in the iTunes algorithms for the first week of the launch, the older show bumped down in the ranks and the newer show came up in the ranks. However, now that we're in the third week, the old show came back to its prior ranking, which is typically top 10 in the marketing category.
>
> The new show is probably now in the top 50 in the marketing category, so we're okay with that; because one of the things, Paul, that we're discovering and what's really fun about what we're doing is we are embedding the show into the article *before* it goes live on the podcast.
>
> What I mean by that is, we already have a bunch of articles on Social Media Examiner that have future episodes of the show, live, which someone can listen to. Then what that does is it gives us a chance to promote our conference, because we have an ad for our conference in the middle of every show.
>
> It also gives people who come to our website a chance

to realize that we even have a daily show and they can subscribe from the web browser, if you will. It's really cool because frankly, I have instructed our editorial team that the second we get the final recordings, we need to immediately embed them into the articles. In fact, we've seen in some articles thousands of listens before the actual podcast has even gone live.

Paul Colligan:

I wouldn't doubt that at all and with the whole nature of the mobile device now, if I am reading your site and there is an article I'm interested in and there's a click-to-play button, I'm going to do that immediately and I might not even subscribe.

Especially if it's the first time of listening to it and I don't even know that there's even a subscription option. So, potentially, that might tweak the subscription numbers which many of us believe are part of the iTunes algorithm anyway, so I think that all comes together quite intelligently. Of course, the iTunes number; that's one number. The true number is the downloads.

Michael Stelzner:

Absolutely.

Paul Colligan:

The true number is the consumption. What are you

seeing? What do you like? You are early in the game and there aren't a lot of people following, so you don't have the benefit of two years of membership.

Michael Stelzner:

I'll give you the number. We've had about 34,000 downloads in the first two weeks and a day.

Paul Colligan:

There we go.

Michael Stelzner:

That's a pretty good number.

Paul Colligan:

Yeah.

Michael Stelzner:

Of those downloads, a pretty significant portion of them are definitely coming from iTunes but also, a significant portion are coming from our actual website itself. I'm searching while we're talking to try to find the actual source stats, but working from memory, I remember that it was probably about 55% was coming from some sort of an iTunes related audience and 45% was coming from elsewhere.

A big chunk of those were from browsers like Chrome and Firefox and Mozilla, so I know that our blog itself is driving a pretty significant portion of the total downloads.

Paul Colligan:

Makes sense.

Michael Stelzner:

We don't really care, right? Because here is our strategy, Paul: we're going to find new people in the iTunes directory and we're going to find new people who come looking at our articles and realize they can consume an audio version; so, the hope would be that they do hit that subscription button - and we do tell them how to do that right there in the article, how to subscribe.

We even link to a video that shows them how to do it in every single article right there after the play button, but in the end, it increases our time on site for those who are there. Our average time on site is three minutes. This is increasing that time dramatically, for those that are listening.

Paul Colligan:

There we go. There we go.

Michael Stelzner:

There are a lot of benefits attached to doing this audio, or re-purposing this content, if you will, into audio.

Paul Colligan:

Of course, the more time on site, the higher the rankings on Google. That's a huge thing now, so the higher the rankings, the more the chance that they are going to bring new people to you who are going to click the play button to hear the audio for the first time to eventually subscribe.

It's a neat little loop, if you will. I wanted to have this conversation because what's so vital here is that you are doing a strategically thought-out, purposeful SOP-driven process for a podcast where it's not you getting in front of the microphone.

Michael Stelzner:

Absolutely.

Paul Colligan:

This is key, because a lot of people think that podcasting must be all of them, all of the time; and you even tried that with the last show, doing them two at a time (although that wasn't the only variable by any means), which was just a lot.

What is it like knowing that another podcast is happening in the office and you don't get to speak every word? Is it hard to give that away?

Michael Stelzner:

It's so liberating, you don't even know.

Paul Colligan:

There we go. There we go.

Michael Stelzner:

We are not a one-man show obviously, right? We've got a pretty nice staff, which affords us the ability to do something like this and it's not cheap. There is a huge amount of labor which goes into doing this, but it's really nice to know that my editorial team has handled 100% of this and I don't need to do anything except just listen every morning when I'm shaving.

It's taken us a long time to get to this point. It was at least a couple months in planning, but we've got the complete system in place and it's working. My hope is that it continues to grow over time and that we tend to grow an audience. For us, we see the big benefit to this is the ability to promote our shows, our conferences or our online shows, right in the middle of our podcast.

It's huge for us because if people love it, they're going

to keep listening and a little 30-second blip in there about the show is only going to help us communicate to our audience that hey, we're more than just content, here.

Down the road, we might sell sponsorships and that kind of thing. I don't have any clue just yet, but it is really intriguing. I don't know if we'll ever show back up in the top rankings for this show, but if we don't, I'm okay with it.

We have many different places on our site where people can discover more about the show. For example, in the navigation bar at the top, we changed it to say "Podcasts," and when you click on it, we show both of our shows with a sample audio clip from each of the shows, as well as all of the different ways you can subscribe.

We put banner ads on the side. We'll eventually add an email into all of our responder campaigns to feed the show to people who have been email subscribers for a couple of weeks. For us, all the signs are very, very positive.

Paul Colligan:

If I am an existing podcaster, I've seen great reach and I'm looking at the possibility for a secondary show, maybe the... I once heard Jim Louderback from Revision3 call the shorter episodes "snackersodes".

I heard you use the word snack so I went back to that. Some people are considering this, though one thing which has stopped people from podcasting is the fear of their own voice in a microphone.

You and I both would respond with a loud: "Get over it!" However, if you can't get over it, is it viable? We hear about podcasting and how it needs to be personal, it needs to be intimate, it needs to be our own voice.

Michael Stelzner:

It doesn't need to be, Paul. Just look at all the popular podcasts and all these other things which are coming on the horizon. They are about telling other people's stories and technically, the personality behind it is irrelevant, right?

As long as the personality has a good voice and can keep the flow going, it's really about the content and so many podcasts today are just people blabbing non-stop about their opinions. There are very few shows out there that are rich, how-to stuff. It's almost unheard of, frankly.

Almost all podcasts are interviews or are someone talking into the microphone for 30 to 45 minutes, sharing their thoughts on things. There are very few shows that I have come across (or at least that I subscribe to) that are very short, under 10 minutes, and actually have a lot of really high-end tactical stuff.

What's unique about Social Media Examiner is, we put $1,000 into development *after* the article comes in, and that goes into every article we publish on Social Media Examiner. That's not taking into account whatever it costs to pay the writer; that's just all the development we do once that article comes into our editorial process.

Our articles are so good (that's why millions of people read them) that I just finally came to the conclusion, "Man, if we could translate this into audio, we could come up with something that, quite frankly, has never been done before."

What I would say to your listeners is that if there is some really, really rich stuff out there that you know about and you can figure out and you write articles about it all the time and those articles tend to become really popular, why not figure out a way to translate it into audio? Because you know what? It only takes about 10 minutes to read 1,000 words.

Paul Colligan:

And it can be 10 minutes of someone else's time.

Michael Stelzner:

Correct.

Paul Colligan:

So it's even less if you...

Michael Stelzner:

I'll be honest, it's very hard to read and not sound like you're reading. You have to be extremely well-trained to do that. I can do it, but I can only do it for so long and to do it for 10 minutes straight is extremely hard for almost anybody. If you've ever been in front of a camera and you try to do a 10-minute video shoot without any takes, it's almost impossible, right?

Paul Colligan:

Exactly, but the beautiful part...

Michael Stelzner:

That's where talent comes in, right?

Paul Colligan:

Exactly; and talent needs to be paid for, but the great thing is that you're promoting a show with a reasonable but respectable ticket price, where you can actually pay for this stuff due to the profits of what it is that you are doing. Is this play only for a big guy? Can a small person do this, or do you have to have $1,000 per episode?

Michael Stelzner:

It depends... no, I'm not spending $1,000 for each episode. I'm spending $1,000 for each article that is published on Social Media Examiner; so our actual cost of this show is about a $30,000 to $40,000 annual investment, okay?

Paul Colligan:

Okay.

Michael Stelzner:

In our case, that involves the cost of the editor to translate the text into audio that will work, the cost of the voice talent, the cost of the production company to sew the whole thing together, the cost of the crew to go ahead and encode and upload everything and to add them to the articles and all that stuff. There are about four or five people doing little bits and pieces, if you will, so that's our cost.

Paul Colligan:

$30k to $40k... but an existing content library that you're pulling from.

Michael Stelzner:

If you divide that 52 times, right? I mean, you divide that by 52 weeks and it's...

Paul Colligan:

Very reasonable.

Michael Stelzner:

It's pretty reasonable if you can develop the kind of audience that you want to develop; and in our case, this is a media play, so we are developing a brand new media channel. If we can get to the point where we have hundreds of thousands of downloads a month, which I think we can very easily get to in the next few months... if that equates to, let's say, 10,000 listeners per episode, that is something we can do enormous things with and every time we have something, anything to promote, these are people that every day are snacking on this content and that just gives us an incredible opportunity to be able to sell more of what we care about.

Paul Colligan:

Absolutely. What's next?

Michael Stelzner:

That is all for podcasting in the near future, at least. Other than Social Media Marketing World.

Paul Colligan:

Of course, of course.. but you are going to try to go to five days a week?

Michael Stelzner:

Oh yeah. It's late January as of this recording. In February, we hope to get to the point where by the middle of the month, we are publishing five days a week and that's where we'll rest. Right now, it's Monday through Thursday and then my other show is on Friday.

We want to get to the point where we are Monday through Friday. I don't really know what percentage of the other show is tuning in to this show. It will be interesting to see in the grand scheme of things if it hurts us or if it helps us, but this is a grand experiment, Paul, and I've never really seen anybody do what we're doing.

My hope is that it works and we'll keep doing it and hopefully a lot of other people will see what we're doing and they'll try it out themselves.

Paul Colligan:

I haven't seen it either, and that's why I asked to do this interview with you - because I wanted to pick your brain. It's funny (and sad), so many podcast interviews are like, "Why are you doing this?" and it's like, "Well you know, we just thought we'd try to see what works." You've got some thought and you've got some purpose and some attention in this that is fun to watch; and of course, the execution is always such a big part of it.

I know that you'll take this as far as you need to go and experiment with it and the beautiful part is, Mike, your decision on whether or not you keep Friday or if you decide that it gets in the way of the other show - that will be a business decision, not an emotional decision or a voting decision from an informal survey to people on Twitter or something like that.

You are building a business here. You've thought it through and you are rejecting some of the traditional expectations of what a podcast is, but you're seeing some great results from doing so. I really appreciate your leadership in the industry, I really appreciate what you're doing here and it's fun to watch and now I too have something to listen to while I shave, so thanks so much. Any final words to the audience here?

Michael Stelzner:

I hope they'll check it out. It's called the ***Social Media Examiner Show***; please, let us know what you think.

Online Marketing Made Easy With Amy Porterfield

Amy Porterfield is a dear friend, former co-worker, and host of a very popular podcast that I also mention in my "Podcasts I Listen To" chapter. Listen to what Amy says, she has this way of making things easy.

Even though it's been around for more than ten years, podcasting has recently exploded in the public consciousness. Audiences drawn in by the runaway success of ever so popular "Serial" podcast are now finding a huge catalogue of audio content tailored to every interest—storytelling, yes, but also news, comedy, music, food and, of course, advice of every kind imaginable...especially the kind oriented toward doing business online.

I started my podcast "Online Marketing Made Easy" to get helpful, valuable and actionable content into the hands of an audience that might not have found me before.The kind who might not spend much time on social networks or search out specific information online, but enjoy coming across great content by following the rabbit trail of podcast categories.

To my surprise, podcasting has become my #1 platform to deliver this kind of content, even to people who have never subscribed to a podcast before.

As a result, podcasting has not only allowed me to deliver valuable, useful content, but has proved a great way for me to grow my email list with quality leads who are genuinely interested in my content. They hear what I have to say; learn new strategies and tips (delivered in my own voice and adding a new level of genuine connection), get engaged and want to know more. I tell them where to click and, while adding value, I am able to grow my email list with quality leads.

No Expertise Required

Podcasting can seem daunting to those who have never tried it. All that fancy equipment! All that production time!

In reality, though, you don't need a tricked-out studio or sophisticated programming know-how to deliver valuable content to your audience. It's as easy as hitting a button and starting a conversation with your audience.

Just like any form of online marketing, the thing that really makes for an effective podcast is getting grounded in what you have to offer.

What is your voice?

What niche do you add value to the most?

Who is your audience and what do you offer that resonates best with them?

These questions get answered through doing, as opposed to thinking about it.

That's why the key to having an effective podcast lies in your process.

What My Process Looks Like

1. **Research and Outline** Everyone suffers from overwhelm, in the early stages of a new endeavor. The sheer volume of things to talk about in your podcast can make it hard to start. Embrace the overwhelm and simply start writing topics—as many as you can think of.

    This is what I did, with the help of a content manager I hired to help me develop the podcast. Between the two of us, we narrowed a list of 50 topics down to four episodes for January, four more for February, and so on, noting down new ideas on the initial list as we cross out old ones. We batch the content to make it easier for us to get the job done.

    For each episode, the content manager fleshes out the initial topic with lots of research. Next, I give her feedback on where the podcast should go. She puts together an outline that leaves plenty of room for me to elaborate and go off on tangents. I take that outline and use it as a base for the recorded podcast--with lots of personal conversational flourishes.

    You might not be ready to hire a content manager, but the process of batching your episodes to get a few done in just a few days, goes a long way, even if you are a one-man or one-woman show.

2. **Recording and Editing** It's rare that a podcast benefits

from being broadcast as is—just a rough, raw audio file. If you've ever tried to tell a story on a recording, you know that there are awkward beats, lost trains of thought, and coughs...lots of coughs.

Once I'm done recording the podcast, I use Dropbox to transfer the files to an audio editor who cuts out the awkward parts and sets up the polished recording to publish on Libsyn and iTunes. I always tell him to not edit "too much" so that I still sound real and raw - like I am talking to a friend. He also uploads it to play directly on my website—for this we use Smart Podcast Player, which is available from Pat Flynn of Smart Passive Income. — and then we have an editor who edits and then sets up things via Libsyn and itunes

3. **The Lead Magnet** By the end of 2014, after a year's worth of podcasts, I decided to change my format. I decided to give the podcast a greater purpose: in addition to offering great content to my existing audience and attracting new people who might not have found me through my previous channels, I started approaching the podcast as a list builder.

   To that end, I started offering a valuable giveaway within each episode, in the form of a downloadable item (checklist, cheat sheet, how-to guide, etc.) that goes into greater depth on the topic discussed in the podcast. I always mention the giveaway a few times within the episode and offer to email it to any listeners who want it.

This, as you may know, is known as a lead magnet—an item of value given in exchange for contact information. This allows me to grow my email list and cultivate a stronger relationship with my audience.

The lead magnet is even easier for podcast listeners to access when I use LeadPages, an online tool that makes downloads available through text message as well as directly from the Internet. For example, in Episode #42 of my podcast, I mentioned midway through the episode that I'd put together a cheat sheet that listed the pros and cons of five major bulk email providers.

I told listeners that they could download my cheat sheet by going to the URL amyporterfield.com/42download (where they would see an opt-in box) or by texting "42download" to 38470. Both methods send the download directly to my listeners email address ...and also gave me new names and addresses to add to my list. (I use the tool Call Loop to add the SMS feature to my show.)

In addition, I've added another layer to my podcast by adding LeadPages as a sponsor to my show. They are not a traditional sponsor where they pay me a few thousand dollars to promote them per episode, but instead I've created a mini LeadPages training (www.amyporterfield.com/newleads) that I promote on all my shows. The mini-training guides my listeners through the process of connecting their own lead magnet to an opt-in box, making it easy for them to build their email list quickly. It's working exceptionally well!

4. **The Blog Post** Rather than simply update my blog with the podcast player and call it a day, I choose to develop a unique blog post around the same topic.

   At first, I tried creating it almost word-for-word from the podcast transcript, but that seemed like it was defeating the purpose of the podcast and made the post feel awkward. Now we create a blog post that serves as a teaser for the podcast—it offers the main talking points of the podcast, along with lots of hints that you can learn so much more if you listen to the episode in full. It's incredible valuable as a standalone post, but more valuable if you listen to the podcast.

   We also use the blog post to promote the lead magnet—another place where we use LeadBoxes, a special feature of LeadsPages. You code the LeadBox into the blog post (super easy to do) and when readers click on it, it brings up a pop-up prompt to enter their email address in exchange for the valuable freebie.

   The final piece of the blog post is a custom image that we commission from a graphic artist on 99designs. It's different every time—a unique, eye-catching piece of typographic art that helps the title of the blog post really stick. This featured image gives a clean, stylish finish to the entire project, and it helps with the final step in the process. Here's an example:

First, the reader sees this option:

To help you with this, I'm offering a special free download—a cheat sheet that shows the opportunities and limitations of some of the most popular email service providers. You can download it for free by clicking here. Or simply text 42download to 38470 and I'll send you that cheat sheet right away.

CLICK HERE TO INSTANTLY DOWNLOAD OUR NEWEST CHEAT SHEET, "TOP EMAIL SERVICE PROVIDERS: PROS AND CONS."

And when they click on the yellow image, they get the opt-in box:

Almost there; please complete this form and click the button below to gain instant access.

Enter Your Email Address Below to Get Your Free Cheat Sheet:
"Top Email Providers: Pros and Cons"

AmyTester

Amyprivate@amyporterfield.com

FREE INSTANT ACCESS »

We hate SPAM and promise to keep your email address safe.

This strategy has resulted in thousands of new leads from my blog post.

5. **Social Media Podcasts** that take off the way Serial did owe their wild popularity to social media. What good is great content if nobody's telling their friends about it?

Our social media promotion is anchored by the featured image from our blog post—I create updates around those images and set them up (using a program called Edgar) to publish on Facebook and Twitter at staggered times throughout the month. I also use the images on Pinterest and Instagram.

Here's an example of a podcast featured image:

All of my social media teasers contain a link back to the podcast episode. The essential thing with social isn't getting people to click "like"—it's to bring them on over to the website, wowing them with a treasure trove of great content, and enticing them to opt in for more.

At the End of the Day

In addition to all the benefits it offers your online marketing campaign, podcasting is just really fun! It allows you to communicate in a natural, off-the-cuff way with your listeners, as if you were having a beer together and talking shop.

It also gives you the opportunity to reconnect with experts in your field through interviews and round-table discussions, which means you get to learn alongside your audience.

Best of all, the podcasting arena still has lots of space for new personalities and perspectives. Now is the perfect time to get in the ring and let your voice be heard.

To hear how one podcaster gets it done (and learn some fresh insights about online marketing) subscribe to my podcast "Online Marketing Made Easy" on iTunes. It would be my pleasure to help you get even bigger results with your online marketing strategies!

Amy Porterfield:

Amy is the co-author of Facebook Marketing All-In-One for Dummies and the creator and host of the top-rated podcast, Online Marketing Made Easy. Before building her online training business, Amy worked with mega brands like Harley-Davidson Motorcycles and Peak Performance Coach, Tony Robbins. Named one of Forbes Top 50 Social Power Influencers, Amy has empowered over 15,000 entrepreneurs, small business owners, coaches and consultants all over the world with her social media marketing training programs.

Why Grow a Podcast Audience When You Can Buy One (With Ed Rush)?

Ed is a friend and coworker/conspirator on a number of projects I'm working on. When he jumped into podcasting, he did so with his typical ALL-IN approach and had some great results with an angle for building an audience that I simply hadn't heard of before - HE BOUGHT THEM. Here's Ed, explaining what he did and why he did it.

I was listening to an old Gary Howard seminar. Gary Howard is a well-known direct copywriter who passed away about three years ago. When he was teaching, people started asking questions like: "How do you have a business structure in LLC?" "What are your recommendations on how to set up a bank account?" He answered, "If I give you a million dollars right now and said that by tomorrow you have to have both your business and your bank account set up, you would figure out how to do it."

It's interesting what you said about microphones, recording and editing and all those similar things we tend to put first, when really those things should be last. The real question we should worry about is: "How am I going to get people to listen to this and engage in my podcast?" I'll tell you what I did. I started a fishing podcast, called *The World's Greatest Fishing Podcast* (http://h2plink.com/WorldsGreatest). We just passed 30,000 downloads this past month and we're growing extremely fast.

I haven't bought every single one of my listeners... but I have bought the majority of them.

Actually, the term "bought" sounds shady and unethical. What we actually mean by "bought" is that I spent advertising dollars to get in front of my market, by using advertising platforms. This audience would have found out about my podcast eventually; it would just have probably been two or three years later. My rule is: "Why should I wait three years to do something, when I can do it in three months?" In the end, I get the benefit of both strategies. There are some screenshots I would like to share with you that are examples of where we actually spent money on promoting. Going back to what I said earlier, the precise number is 31,455 downloads of the podcast in this month.

We use a lot of Facebook, Twitter and Instagram marketing. We haven't paid for anything on Instagram; we just share and interact a lot with our followers. We do have a lot of traffic from Instagram, and that's very encouraging because it's free. The traffic from Twitter is also free, but the traffic from Facebook is a mix of free and paid. It's also a mix of those whom we paid to get us likes, who ended up coming to our advertorial list and who originated with an ad. Now though, it's more organic.

Here's an example of the best thing about Facebook: we did an episode with a guy named Jim Sammons, a kayak and fishing expert who is pretty popular online, especially on Facebook. So, we ran an ad with his photograph on our podcast with a line that said "Is it possible to fish and kayak at the same time?"

We ran an ad specifically to the people who follow him. We ended up with 45 shares of that particular ad, because all of his fans saw him in their news feed. I asked him to put something on his social media about the show, but he didn't do it. I think he just forgot, but when he saw the ad that I ran, he shared it with his audience. In the end, we got ourselves a lot of traffic from that ad, simply because of sharing.

Originally, I didn't even have a show; I just knew I would have one, but I wanted to gain some followers first. I started a Facebook page with two likes in January and by the first week of March we had a little over 20,000 fans on that page. Those fans were mostly paid. We're still doing a "like" campaign. We just run an ad on the right side of the news feed. It was easy to find people who are interested in fishing, because most people who like fishing actually say that they do in their interests and that's how we targeted them. We started ads that we thought would be appropriate for fishermen and clicking on it meant that they liked our page and then they started interacting with us. We were doing that for anywhere between five and 15 cents per like. What that means is that we built a following of over 20,000 people for less than $2,000 dollars.

Currently, I've spent nearly $10,000 dollars towards building my audience - which is a total of six months, all-in. I don't really know the exact number, but on launch day I probably put about $1,500 dollars into my ad account because we were trying to make some downloads on iTunes. We ended up number one in the Outdoor and Sports category and number twenty-four in Overall, beating Rachel Bada, Dave Ramsey and a lot of ESPN shows. That was a proof of concept for me, as well.

Similarly, there are people who try to do the same thing i.e. building an audience, but they will target people in Cambodia and Vietnam. That kind of following is completely worthless to them. For me, Facebook numbers were not important. I was actually looking for people who will download and subscribe to my podcast. To get that, I needed real people who are interested in fishing. Those people are mostly from USA, Canada, UK and Australia. The majority were native English speaking, 90% male between 25 and 55 years old. The average time on Facebook is almost all day, basically from 9 AM to 9 PM. We know a lot about our market. We know who they are and that they're actual fishermen (part of our audience are fisherwomen, too). The reason we did that precise targeting is because we needed people who would respond to following our marketing messages for us.

This week the average download number per week is 1,600, which is quite good. Moreover, the important thing is that I've dialed down the amount spent on Facebook, even though our numbers are spiking. This is partly because we're getting the benefit of a lot of organic reach from Facebook, Instagram and Twitter, enabling us to move where we want to move. This is also how we've built our email list, which is very helpful. Once the flow is perfect, we're going to do about three or four ads per show.

To be honest, I literally had no idea why I started this. I was interested in fishing and I loved the idea of not just doing something, but being well-known in market place for doing it. So, while we were starting it, I just wanted to see what we could do in the market and we have picked up some great results along the way. For example, the first show I did with Michael Fowlkes, executive producer of a show called *Inside Sportfishing* on Fox Sports, opened up an opportunity. After the show, we started talking and eventually we ended up discussing his book, which I was able to help him out a little bit with. Later, we ended up agreeing to have lunch together in San Diego. He walked into that restaurant and said, "I love your stuff. I want to do a TV show with you guys." One and a half months later, we were sitting in San Diego bay, on a boat that we had borrowed from Fisherman's Landing, one of the biggest fishing stores in San Diego, filming a show for Fox. Only a year before that, I had barely ever caught a fish in town. Recently, we created a course together that is launching next month. It's about how to catch a halibut - a fish we catch here in San Diego. That is going to be another stream of income for us.

I got the call yesterday from Dennis Westminster, who has a show on World Fishing Network, about wild fishing and wild places. He called me yesterday and said, "Hey, I want to pitch a joint sponsorship deal with you." This is a method of penetrating the market in a way that nobody else knows how to do.

For another example, the biggest and brightest names in fishing all have television shows right now. It's safe to say that none of them are thinking about doing a podcast, but the majority of them understand online or digital marketing. In the world of digital advertising, all the sponsors are starting to ask questions about real numbers. Someone who is on TV, for example, will ask about their subscriber base and the response will most probably be that agencies estimate they are having 70,000 viewers per episode. However, sponsors are going to say that they don't believe much in those numbers. They might ask "What are your real numbers?" The most interesting thing about having a digital marketing arm, whether it's Facebook, Twitter or Instagram, is that you can always quantify your audience in real-life numbers. For instance, when you have a podcast download - that is a real number. When I was talking to Dennis, he remarked that it is all true and that they are really looking for real numbers. Part of the play, also, is being able to combine media with media to create bigger deals and bigger sponsorships. That is where we are moving right now; we are heading in that direction.

So, for all those out there who are just starting out or who have a concept and are just thinking about launching their own podcast, the first thing that you have to keep in mind is that podcasting is essentially free. It is not free in terms of your time, but if you want to get something syndicated on iTunes, you can do it with very little expense. What I recommend, because I've have been teaching podcasting for a while now, is just to get it up and going. Get it started and get it out there. Okay, someone might say "Wait a second, I only have eight weeks to be on a new network and I need it to have it all done." No, you don't need to have it all done. In fact, I am getting ready to start two more shows, one of which could end up being my big marketing show, but I did that because I started to learn that there is so much interest in this area of fishing and I would never have known that if it wasn't for this particular show. You have to learn a lot faster; you go faster through the motions, not through the meditation.

Furthermore, if you are thinking about starting a podcast, now is the time to do it. Grab a microphone, do a couple of interviews, record it and get it out there. Don't worry about the name, just get it up on iTunes and you will learn more from doing that than from thinking about it for a couple of months or planning it for another couple of months. If you are already experienced, most of us get to the point when we realize that there are not enough people listening and not enough people interacting. This can all get to the point where it starts being a little frustrating, honestly. I was there for the first two months, when there was 7,000 or 8,000 downloads and we were trying really hard to make it bigger. Finally, all of a sudden it took off and exploded.

My recommendation for everyone who is doing a podcast (or any other show or business out there) is this: every single month, just put in one more way to get new leads, new downloads or new subscribers. When I started out, all I had was a Facebook page and a blog. At that point, I didn't even have a show on iTunes yet. Then in March, we launched our show on iTunes, in April we started using Instagram and in late May we started on Twitter. Those were the things that we added one at a time, so that we could see what was happening. We could then figure out what was working and what wasn't. We could tell what kind of interaction, what kind of posting and what kind of commenting was working for us. Besides that, we also started to see this momentum building from Facebook followers, Instagram followers and all these others and we began to realize the value of multimedia. We had our email list, as well as Facebook, Instagram and Twitter followers, and if someone started following us on all of these three places, the chances of us seeing a syndicated podcast were just getting bigger.

If you are planning on doing this for a while, all that I am saying is that every month, you should add more ways of getting new leads, new downloads and new subscribers in your marketing plan. Give it a try and if it doesn't work, don't do that anymore. But, if it does work, you might find that you are suddenly going from 8,000 or 10,000 followers to 30,000 in one month, like I did - because you will start finding new ways of engaging your lead base.

If you want more details, just go to http://h2plink.com/WorldsGreatest. There is plenty of contact information on our website and there you can see all of the other things that we are doing with this show.

Ed Rush

Ed is a former Marine Corps F-18 pilot and fishing enthusiast. While he knows a ton about fishing, he also freely acknowledges that he's the guy who often gets his gear jammed and spends much of his time on the water un-fouling his lines. His passion is kayak fishing with his kids, who are five, six and eight years old, respectively.

How I Created The World's #1 Medical Tourism Podcast From Scratch In Under 90 days (With John Cote)

As you can tell from this article, I've known John for some time now. He's a go-getter like few others I know and when we jumped into the podcasting space, I knew he would be a force to content with. What he's done (and in such a short amount of time) has been amazing and anyone reading this has plenty to learn from him.

My "What What" moment on how to rapidly create digital media.

I was fortunate to meet Paul at a live event in San Diego about 3 years ago. During the presentation, he mentioned how he had rapidly created and published a Kindle book by recording his thoughts into his iPhone, getting them transcribed and edited and then published. I was absolutely blown away by the simplicity of this concept. I thought it took years and a lot of hard work to publish a book. On the drive home from the airport and a couple of roundtrips thereafter, I did exactly what he talked about. I outlined the book in my head and had eleven chapters in mind. I turned on my voice recorder app and just started talking. We hired out the art-work and formatting and handled the editing in house. Within 6 weeks, I had my first book published on Amazon and it became a #1 best seller on Amazon. That led to more speaking engagements and new clients for my marketing agency.

Because of that book, I was asked to speak at a medical tourism conference in 2013. Just before I went to that conference, I heard Paul talking about podcasting and how easy it was to get started in that medium. I took that to heart and added a slide in my keynote to cover it. While I was onstage, I mentioned to the attendees that podcasting was really taking off and explained why they should consider creating their own podcast. I shared with them that when I searched iTunes, there were no medical tourism shows and that there was a huge opportunity for any of them to own the space. As with many things in life, most people thought it was a great idea, but no one took action.

After several months I decided to create my own show that interviewed patients who had traveled for medical procedures along with Doctors, and medical experts from around the world. We started the process in February 2014 and my goal was to launch in 10 weeks. Before that conference, I didn't really know anything about medical tourism nor did I know much about podcasting. But, I did know how to tell a story and get it distributed globally via the internet. My intent was to share their success stories in a compelling manner to help educate and inspire people about what was possible. At that point I became an advocate and educator for all things medical tourism. I invested time educating myself about the industry, where the common destinations and procedures were, and why people were doing this. From that information I created a series of questions to ask, then started looking for people to interview.

I had met a large number of people at the conference and many of them opted in to my texting campaign in exchange for a copy of my Keynote slides. I reached out to them and started setting up appointments to interview them for the show. The response was impressive; the vast majority of them saw the value and benefit in sharing their story and their patient's stories. I also reached out to several Facebook groups of people who were traveling for medical reasons and landed quite a few very high quality interviews.

Rapid Branding with Crowdsourcing

I got together with my mastermind group and started working on a brand name and title for the show. The name Healthcare Elsewhere came up pretty quickly and we all agreed that was what we were looking for. I sent that name out to a 99 Designs competition and about a week later, we had our logo. It's easy to spend way too much time and money on this and I wanted to focus on the content. We rapidly went through this stage and created a brand that seems to resonate with our listeners with minimal time and money spent. I then created social media profiles and set up the automation to post the episodes to them when they went live. This was very helpful in the launch process.

Podcast Production - KISS

We kept it as simple as possible at this point. I bought a microphone and a preamp and used Skype with a $30 plugin (Call Recorder) to record the interviews. I had speaking experience but no formal training on how to interview people.

I listened to other successful shows for some ideas and just decided to be myself during the interview. It took me a few episodes to get a feel for the show and what I thought would be interesting to the listeners. I asked for input via social media to find out what types of stories people were interested in. Many of the stories we recorded were incredible and very heartwarming. People were overcoming a variety of severe difficulties both medically and financially. Their stories helped create compelling content which led to listeners sharing the show via social media along with some interesting discussions online.

After I had about thirty interviews completed, we launched on April 21st, 2014. I had set a launch date at the beginning and I feel that is important to give yourself a sense of urgency. This really helped me focus on what was important to reach my self imposed deadlines. We debuted at #1 in two of our iTunes categories in New and Noteworthy on launch day because we had planned and executed our launch strategy that others in the book will be talking about.

Once we had a dozen episodes published, I started reaching out to leading industry experts and best selling authors to interview on the show. Don't be afraid to reach out to anyone no matter how famous, the worst they can say is no. Be polite and persistent. I use an online scheduling app to let the subject set their own interview time based on my availability. They can also change the interview times if needed which saves you both time from playing email and phone tag. I automate as much as possible and this can be a real time saver.

We started out as a daily show for the first two months to rapidly build content for the book. We have been posting twice a week on Mondays and Thursdays since then and that seems to be working fine. A daily show takes a lot of effort, make sure you take a look at your end goal when you decide how often you will produce a show. We hired a professional voice artist to do our intro's, midroll's and outro's. Be sure to add a call to action at the end of your show to engage the listeners. We have received plenty of compliments about the quality of the show and how it sounds like a "real" show. People have an expectation that podcasts will have professional radio quality so you should strive for that. You can hire people on Fiverr to do voiceovers for just five bucks if your budget is small.

We used to spend some extra time with the editing the raw audio to take out the "uhmm's" and "ahhh's", long pauses, "you know's" etc. Eventually we stopped doing that and pretty much leave the show as is to save time and keep it natural. If you are editing your own show and are just learning how to use audio editing tools, this will save you a ton of time. Remember, perfection is your enemy. Just create the content and distribute it. If you need more confirmation on that just listen to some of the top podcasts and you will hear what I mean.

One other added benefit of being asked to speak at conferences was that it gave me the opportunity to get on the trade show floor and meet a lot of industry contacts and interview them right at their booth. We brought a small, portable dual mic setup so that I could conduct interviews face to face which is a lot of fun. I had a custom branded mic flag so, as show attendees were walking by, they knew who we were. That led to more interviews and some consulting deals as well. You can also look into doing live broadcasts/webinars that can be used as bonus material later on.

Distribution

We believe in putting the show in as many places as possible (You, Everywhere, Now as Paul and Mike like to say.) The show is available on our website and over a dozen podcasting platforms via RSS feed. We also have custom channels on Spreaker and Soundcloud.

Once you start getting yourself out there, you will begin to receive requests for interviews on other shows. With their permission, you can use that content in books, blogs, social media posts and more.

Monetization

Prior to getting started, podcasting was not on my radar. I occasionally listened to an episode but I didn't understand the value from a business perspective until I discovered Paul, Mike Koenigs and John Lee Dumas. When I witnessed what was possible, I took action. I used John's interview format to create my own unique show in a completely different niche. Our goal was to create great content as I said, but also to monetize in multiple ways.

I started this podcast knowing that we would have a ton of great content that I could use for a book. We planned ahead and had thirteen of the episodes transcribed and then turned into the content of my third book. We ran a best seller campaign to promote it and it became an international best seller, reaching #1 in the U.S. We use the books as another positioning tool to further solidify our dominance in this niche. We had Kindle, paperback and hardcover editions published and they are now available "everywhere books are sold."

Since launching, the show has exceeded one million downloads in under 9 months. We are talking with several companies about paid sponsorship. Doctors and medical tourism companies are contacting me for consulting help on how to promote their business with podcasts, books and online content. I have been asked to speak at multiple medical tourism conferences internationally. Overall I would say that it has been well worth the time we put into it.

The Minutiae

Don't get hung up on minutiae. The hosting, equipment, software, website etc. will all come together. The important thing is to create quality content consistently, then promote it to get listeners. Stop thinking about how hard it is (it isn't) and just do it. You can get started with a smartphone. You will not be perfect and that's OK. Accept that and make it happen. My plan was simple and I executed it and you can do the same.

1. Create great story based content and consistently publish it to as many podcast platforms as possible
2. Set up a bunch of interviews in advance and start recording them

3. Promote the show via Facebook, Twitter, and speaking engagements

4. Sign sponsors and consulting clients

5. Shampoo (Lather, Rinse, Repeat)

The rest fell into place because we had planned for success. I hired a Virtual Assistant (VA) from the beginning to handle my podcast production and social media since I needed time to run my company. You don't have to start there, but I recommend you look at that as a goal for the future once you start monetizing.

After 100 episodes I can say that I have a pretty good handle on the subject, but I don't consider myself to be an expert. That's fine with me since I am more interested in interviewing subject matter experts and patients who have been there done that to tell their stories. This provides our listeners with the best possible content with a variety of solutions to similar issues.

You can listen to John's show at www.HealthcareElsewhere.com and you can learn more about the book here www.HealthcareElsewhereBook.com

About John Cote:

John Cote is the Award Winning author of several Amazon.com #1 Best Selling books. His company, John Cote & Associates, develops growth strategies for any size company and creates client marketing platforms using digital marketing and publishing best selling books, podcasts, and online webinars. A voracious reader, John invests a great deal of time researching cutting edge trends in technology, social media and marketing.

His latest project is the Healthcare Elsewhere show, the worlds leading medical tourism podcast where patients share their success stories and he interviews Doctors and healthcare experts worldwide. His most recent book is the International Best Seller based on the show and it's also titled HEALTHCARE ELSEWHERE.

www.JohnCote.net

www.HealthcareElsewhere.com

Make it Digital – BIGG Success (With Mary-Lynn Foster)

I appreciate, deeply, the simplicity offered by Mary-Lynn in this piece. They haven't let technology get in the way of producing more than 1,000 episodes, and neither should you.

We're George and Mary-Lynn from The BIGG Success Show. We've been podcasting since November of 2007. In 2015, we'll hit show number 1,000! Our podcast is in the What's Hot section in iTunes for Business/Careers. In 2012, we got picked up by a radio syndicator.

We get requests from people all the time wanting to see our BIGG recording studio. Really, there's not much to show. Mary-Lynn came from radio broadcasting and worked in fancy professional recording studios, but in podcasting, you don't need all that!

Really, when it comes to podcasting, it's what you say that matters more than how it sounds. What got us a syndicated radio deal wasn't the quality as much as the content and our track record of consistency.

What could you use to capture your message?

- A free conference service that records a phone call

- A free app that records your voice on your phone

Where should you record?

- In a room that doesn't have a lot of echo or background noise

That's it!

Remember, the quality of your content trumps the quality of your audio production.

Find the BIGG Success Show on:

BIGG Success:

http://biggsuccess.com/podcast-2/

iTunes:

http://phobos.apple.com/WebObjects/MZStore.woa/wa/vie wPodcast?id=269019283

Stitcher:

http://www.stitcher.com/podcast/bigg-success-podcast-feed?refid=stpr

Tunein:

http://tunein.com/radio/The-Bigg-Success-Show-p415143/

About The BIGG Success Show Hosts: George Krueger and Mary-Lynn Foster

George Krueger is a serial business owner who also teaches entrepreneurship at the University of Illinois. Mary-Lynn Foster is a veteran radio show host turned social media entrepreneur. She is also a renowned voice-over talent and audio producer. On the BIGG Success Show, you'll get the information and inspiration you need to live your life on your own terms. Find us online at: http://biggsuccess.com Find all the places to subscribe to our show on our podcast page: http://biggsuccess.com/podcast-2

How I Use the Four Elements of Podcasting (With Fred Castaneda)

Fred was a student of mine in the early days of podcasting and hasn't looked back since. His tenacity in this space is something we can all aim for.

Although I started consuming podcasts with a passion in 2005, it was 2006 when I launched my first podcast show and episodes. I had listened to Paul Colligan's "***Podcast Tools***" weekly show, but I had not met him in person yet. I have to give credit where credit is due. When I decided to create my digital media and publish my podcast in iTunes and elsewhere, I used the four-step formula that was delivered by Scott Whitney in his podcast called "***Podcasting for Business***," which has now podfaded. The four-step formula was plan, produce, publish & promote your podcast. This is the formula that I used -- and to a certain degree, it is similar to Paul Colligan's four elements in his book, "How To Podcast."

I started with a single podcast in 2006, and since then, my passion and obsession led me to produce and publish eighteen podcasts, eight of which are currently still active. My flagship podcast, "The Struggling Entrepreneur," was actually one of the very first podcasts that interviewed entrepreneurs, a genre that is being copied by almost everyone today. In fact, I had Paul Colligan as an interviewee in 2007 in episode 10; I am on episode 260 at the time of this writing.

My other key podcasts are: "***Skills in Screencasts and Podcasts***," at www.SkillsInScreencastsAndPodcasts.com;

"Podcast Reporter" at www.podcastReporter.com, which was inspired from Paul Colligan's *"The Podcast Report"*; *"Boomers for Startups"* at www.boomersforstartups.com; *"Finance for Startups"* at www.finance4startups.com; and *"Entrepreneur Tools Online"* at www.entrepreneurtoolsonline.com. I have podfaded 10 podcast shows since 2006. I was a podcaster that had no delay in creating and publishing a show when my passion took over. As a matter of fact, I even created a show that was inspired by Paul Colligan 2009 called *"Community of Five Podcast."*

Since then, I have become what Paul Colligan describes as a "luminary" in the podosphere, and I have been a speaker at the Social Media Telesummit, Blogworld, New Media Expo, and various Podcamps nationwide since 2007. I have been a Meetup organizer for the Austin, Texas Podcasters Group, and I have been a follower of Paul Colligan with his New Media Inner Circle, including one of his first students when he offered the "Podcast Secrets" course in 2007, and other programs.But now let me show you how I map my original four steps to podcasting (known in 2006 as the original "4-Ps" to the four elements in Paul's book "How to Podcast."

How I Make Digital Media

I create content wherever I go and in whatever location, format, environment and opportunity there is. Case in point: I recorded every meeting, session, meetup, and seminar that I attended -- to the point that one of my Podcast Users' Meetup attendees said to me as I set up my Zoom H4N and H2 "Wow,

Fred, I can see that no matter where you are, *you are always capturing and creating content.*"

As a trained Project Manager with over 33 years of Corporate Sales and Marketing Business employment, as well as time-management teaching experience, the initial tasks that I perform when I want to create my digital content is to PLAN – by using an episode map. This detailed control spreadsheet allows me to manage multiple podcasts and multiple episodes. That is my secret for being able to create, manage, publish and update so many podcast shows. Anyone can do this and create their own version of an episode map, which some people refer to as an "editorial calendar."

Next I capture or create content: (a) by recording the audio during Meetups or meetings, always with my trusted release form for those whose content I capture, so that I can publish it later; (b) by recording monologues of myself with topics that have content that is of value to my listeners; or (c) by conducting interviews of subject matter experts or interested parties -- for instance, with aspiring entrepreneurs and startups or experienced small business owners for my "Struggling Entrepreneur" podcast. Sometimes I conduct and record interviews with more than just one interviewee. By the way, the latter has received the most complementary feedback and thanks from my listeners than any other -- especially when I had 2 experts in their fields contribute to a topic in "*Skills in Screencasts and Podcasts*" (i.e., Ray Ortega of Podcasters Roundtable and Lon Naylor of Screencast Weekly).

More recently, my digital media has expanded to include screencasts and video. I really backed into this from my consulting services that include not only podcasting, but screencasting and video. By following the approach of "I see you out there" (ISYOT) that Paul Colligan taught with the coining of the phrase, my content was syndicated to many locations on the web. After I do my planning and recording of the audio, I do post-production editing and get the "golden master" mp3 files to publish. By the way, I do save ALL of my versions in uncompressed format; and, yes, I do have a lot of external storage for these archives. Now I am ready to put this media online.

How I Put Digital Media Online

As a systems engineer, I know how to do all the tech tasks myself. But I chose to invest into podcasting in the same way you would invest in a hobby or a business. So I decided that my time was better spent in capturing and creating and preparing content, instead of doing the tech work.

So what did I do? I outsourced the tech to a subject matter expert and services consultant -- Dave Jackson. My podcast / blog site was set up and my feed was created, and, in certain cases, my podcasts were even submitted to iTunes by my outsourced consultant, complete with all the artwork (i.e., the badge and the banners and the album art). I feel that this was one of the smartest things I did. Did it cost some money? Yes, but was it worth it? MOST DEFINITELY.

With my iTunes podcast setup and my blog site on WordPress ready, I myself uploaded the mp3 files. I wrote and included the show notes and the imagery and created a post for every episode in every podcast. And, as WordPress gives you the time stamp function, I was able to schedule the release of my posted episodes in the future at the date and time that I wanted.

Why? Because podcasting time is like creativity; sometimes you get a lot of it at one time, and then your commitments prohibit you from being consistent with gaps of time in the later days or weeks. With this feature of timestamp, I could create, edit, upload, post and publish multiple episodes on the same day as drafts -- but schedule them for release in the future at timed intervals, which then made me consistent to my audience and listeners. This allowed me time to do follow-up thank-you emails to my interviewees, as well as other admin tasks, and also pursue creating more content of value.

How I Get My Digital Media Podcast-Ready

By having outsourced the blog / podcast site creation and the iTunes submission to my consultant as services, the infrastructure is podcast ready. By uploading my digital media as episodes and/or links in my podcast episode posts, which is really the fun part of podcasting to me, I am ready for the podcast to publish. This is done by using the episode map as a plan and the time stamp feature of WordPress to finalize the media as "podcast-ready."

How I Tell the World About My Digital Media in Podcasts

By publishing my podcast episode posts from WordPress and using the timestamp feature, my episode goes out to the iTunes directory. I also have other directories and syndicated locations where I publish the episodes. In addition, I do my own cross-reference and syndication, by repurposing one episode that may be relevant to another podcast show at that site. For instance, an entrepreneur topic in startup finance may be relevant to *"Struggling Entrepreneur," "Boomers for Startups," "Finance for Startups,"* and may merit a discussion in *"Podcast Reporter."* Thus, I have my own ISYOT and syndication repurposing strategy.

For two other podcast shows that are for nonprofits and community service (i.e., veterans service organizations), I do not publish them on iTunes. Since the audience is so niched (e.g., past or present combat infantrymen and paratroopers of the US Army), I rely on my promotion plan for these two shows. This includes restricted comments, as well as viral and targeted promotion via meetings, newsletters and direct contact with the audiences, who are usually the troopers themselves, but mostly their families, friends and loved ones. There is no monetization plan for these two shows dealing with the nonprofit organizations. You may call that my contribution to military and community service.

I do have a promotion plan, which includes email, directories, social media, etc. (the "traditional" ways). But I have found another way that gives better results more quickly. This is by using a business card that I distribute when I meet key people in person about my shows. I made it a point to have a separate business card about each podcast show. Instead of a book or an ebook, which today is called an "expensive business card," I deliver these cards at events since I do attend quite a few.

I get results from email as the word spreads about my shows, and I also have had good results for consulting services that come from listeners or their audiences who want to pursue podcasting or screencasting from my expertise. I have included and attached a sample of the latest business card for "*Skills in Screencasts and Podcasts*" -- I do use back and front and four color, with two lines available to capture name & email.

Finally, I provide interviews to other podcasters. This is what gets me introduced to their audiences (e.g., "The Coachzing" show) and gets me results from others who want to contact me for either services or for interviews. When I do get a chance to submit a bumper of my show for inclusion to another podcast, I take advantage of this, such as I did for Paul Colligan's "*The Podcast Report*" and other previous podcasts that Paul had in 2007. It is so true that nothing is as productive and with a large reach than "word of mouth marketing."

SUMMARY: By outsourcing the tech to someone who can accomplish in ten minutes what would take me forty-five minutes to do, and by keeping the workflow and process simple, I concentrate on the easy and fun tasks of creating content and using an efficient process, much like a well-oiled machine to keep podcasting, which I consider my "out of the box" thinking, on new ways for promotion.

Fred Castaneda

Fred Castaneda is a podcasting, screencasting and video consultant who provides services for entrepreneurs and other small business owners. With his BA and MBA from Loyola University, he spent spent 33 years in Corporate America before he launched as a full-time entrepreneur in New Media -- especially podcasting. With experience and background in TV and Film, Fred has also taught International Business and Dance at the University -- and this he did after serving as a Combat Infantryman and Paratrooper during the Vietnam War. In addition to consulting services, Fred has spoken at different Podcast and social edia conferences, and he now creates and teaches courses in New Media--especially podcasting and screencasting. Fred is grateful to his mentors in this area-- a key one being Paul Colligan.

Key links to my more well-known podcasts:

http://www.PodcastReporter.com

http://www.SkillsInScreencastsAndPodcasts.com

http://www.StrugglingEntrepreneur.com

http://www.FinanceForStartups.com

It's About Time (With Steven Cardinal)

Podcasting isn't always news and interviews - as you can see from Steven.

My name is Steven Cardinal and I am the co-producer of It's About Time (http://itsabouttimetravelagency.com), a biweekly audio drama about two bumbling idiots who discover a time portal in their closet. In their pursuit of fame and fortune, they wreak havoc throughout history while blissfully unaware of the sinister powers that are following in their wake.

A production of The Cardinal James Show (http://cardinaljames.com), which my good friend Charlie James and I created, It's About Time has been getting rave reviews and awesome feedback since we launched in September of 2014. We have received recognition for the quality of the writing as well as the incredible sound editing (courtesy of Charlie).

While producing a show is not without its challenges: writing and refining scripts, scheduling actors for recording sessions, identifying great sound effects and editing, one of the greatest challenges is marketing. Audio dramas are such a small niche and it can be difficult to get people to hear about your show, let alone give it a listen. The advice often given by other podcasters - interview popular people, discuss trending topics - simply is not relevant to us. So, then, how have we grown our listener base seven-fold over the first five episodes? Creating relationships.

The audio drama community is small but passionate and, like most communities, welcoming to new people, but they expect those people to contribute. For It's About Time, it was crucial that we first find the die-hard audio drama listeners and the easiest way to do that was to find the other audio dramas.

By participating in communities such as those on reddit.com, we were able to directly engage people who would be willing to give us a listen. It was not just soliciting listeners, though; it was about participating in the community. We have shared ideas about casting, recording, editing, and marketing, pushed each other, and helped each other. We have taken to social media to be supportive of each other. We have helped each other grow.

For listeners of audio drama there are not enough episodes to quench their thirst for good entertainment. The production of each episode takes considerable time and many producers can only release on a biweekly schedule. That means a listener can subscribe to many shows and enjoy them all. Sharing listeners does not cannibalize your own listeners. Instead, it builds a stronger community that is more passionate.

We have also sought out fans by reaching out to the media that covers our niche. If we find someone writing articles about audio dramas, we will reach out and introduce ourselves. No hard sells or spammy messages, just a brief introduction with links on how to get more information. Think of it as a press release for the Internet age.

Marketing such a niche product is a challenge, but we are

creating something we love and, in the end, this is about scratching that artistic itch and sharing it with the world.

Steve Cardinal

Originally from Massachusetts, Steven now lives in Charleston, SC where he defends the nation's computer systems by day and acts, blogs, and podcasts by night. Co-producer of the hit audio drama, It's About Time, he also co-stars on the relationship podcast: MOD Love. You can find him and his various extracurricular activities at www.straighttalkwithsteve.net.

Making Digital Media With Dave Bullis

I love Dave's brevity here. Making digital media doesn't have to be hard.

The process of creating a podcast can seem daunting at first but if you follow this guide I can show you how easy it is to record a podcast.

Step #1 - The Computer

First you'll need a computer which I assume you have. If you don't, you can reach out to your local library or college to see if they'll let you record using their computers. I'm not going to get into what is better, Mac or Windows, because at the end of the day it really doesn't matter.

Step #2 - The Microphone

Most computers (particularly laptops) come equipped with their own microphones and sometimes cameras too. The reason that it's more important for audio than video is because, when using any video conferencing service, it's more important that you hear the other person than see them. If you'd like you can buy a USB mic. USB mics are relatively cheap and simply plug into the USB port on the side of your computer. Just check before you buy that it's compatible with your computer (Mac or Windows) and your current operating system.

Step #3 - How to Record

Now if you're going to just discuss a topic yourself then everything is very simple.

Download two completely FREE programs.

- Skype: A free and most widely used video conferencing service.

- Audacity: A free recording program.

- If you're going to have a guest then you need to buy the following program:

- Evaer: Evaer lets you record your Skype calls and supports multiple users as well. So if you have four (4) guests on, you will be able to record everyone.

Step #4 - Editing your Audio

Once you're done, you can take the audio file and simply open it in Audacity.

From there you can cut any parts out you don't want, in order to make the recording playback seamlessly.

Step #5 - Intro and Outro's

If you want to get slightly more advanced and up your production value you can add an intro & outro to your podcast. To do this, you can pull in music and sound effects and edit them together. There is a plethora of free sound sites, like FreeSound.org. If you prefer, you can even outsource this work to a site like Fiverr.

You're done! Now onto uploading online.

Dave Bullis
http://DaveBullis.com
http://BullWittMedia.com
Follow Me on Twitter
Friend me on Facebook
Add me on Google Plus

Make Digital Media In Two Different Locations (With Tom Stewart)

Here is another quick approach to making digital media that proves that the process doesn't need to be complicated - even if you aren't in the same physical location.

Our podcast "A Swift Kick in the Ass" consists of myself, Tom Stewart, located in Fort Lauderdale, FL and my best friend, John Curren, located in Richmond, VA.

I will start with John's setup: he uses a podcast-in-a-box solution from Behringer audio which includes a small two-channel audio mixer, microphone, headphones and a USB audio interface to connect the mixer to his computer. The kit had everything he needed to get started for $99 dollars.

John connects with me via Google Hangouts on air, and this is broadcast live and automatically uploaded to our YouTube channel after we stop broadcasting. Since I am a radio broadcast engineer by trade, I handle the more complex setup and recording on my side. I have a fourteen channel mixer which allows me to input fourteen different audio sources and send out two separate outputs. I only use a few inputs: my microphone, audio from my tablet for intro and exit music, and my laptop, which is the audio coming from John via Google Hangouts On Air. My main mixer output feeds a digital recorder and my auxiliary audio (AUX) output feeds my audio to John via a USB audio interface connected to my laptop. Having a mixer with a separate AUX audio feed allows me to create what is called a mix minus; everything John needs to hear (Mix) except himself (Minus). If I did not do it this way, John would immediately throw off his headphones because his own voice would come back to him with a few seconds of delay, creating an annoying echo in his headphones. This is the biggest mistake in broadcasting and it happens all the time to seasoned professionals. A mix minus can be created using software but it is much easier to use a mixer with an auxiliary audio output.

Using Google Hangouts On Air does a few things for us. First, it allows us to place a video (talking head) version of our podcast on YouTube automatically without having to upload it, saving a lot of time. Being on YouTube gets us more exposure and helps us grow our audience. Second, the YouTube version acts as a backup audio source for us. Once we lost an entire episode because I forgot to press the record button, however, we were able to download the mp3 audio file from YouTube which saved our butts. The final benefit is that we are recording live which gives a little more spunk to our presentation. If we make a mistake, we just roll with it and keep moving forward. Our philosophy is to treat it like a live radio show and use as little post-production as possible in order to get the podcast out the door quickly. We have full time jobs and do not want to create another job for ourselves as editors. I even play our pre-produced intro and exit audio from my tablet which sometimes gets fat-fingered and I play the wrong element - big deal. I do drop the audio file into Adobe Audition to cut the head and tail off the recording which is just John and me discussing what we have planned for the show. I add a preset effect to the WAV file called "podcast voice" which automatically corrects the level differences between our voices and then I export the file to a mp3 file, which we upload to our media hosting company, Libsyn. The file is sent to iTunes directly from Libsyn and we use a paid Wordpress plugin called Simple Podcast Press that grabs our RSS feed from iTunes and posts it automatically on our website.

The Podcast:

A Swift Kick in the Ass, is a podcast about positive personal change. The thought provoking show discusses strategies to help the ordinary person achieve extraordinary change. It is hosted by lifelong friends John W. Curren and Tom Stewart who are on a quest to disrupt conventional thinking and find true freedom by living life on their own terms. Find the podcast at www.aswiftkickintheass.com.

About Tom Stewart:

As a United States Air Force veteran, I directly supported the President and the Secretary of Defense aboard the nuclear hardened E-4B known as the "Doomsday Plane". Now I spend my days working in South Florida radio as a broadcast engineer and my evenings rolling around on a mat with my family at a Brazilian Jiu Jitsu gym.

Loudness Normalization and Compression of Podcasts and Speech Audio (With Georg Holzmann of Auphonic.com)

Auphonic has changed the Podcasting game for me dramatically, The automation and audio hacks they bring to the game is nothing short of fantastic. When Georg Holzmann from Auphonic said I could republish these pieces from the Auphonic Blog in my book, I couldn't have been more thrilled.

Where I, and many of you, are happy with a statement of "use Auphonic, it just works," others want an explanation of what goes on behind the scenes are this section does just that. In addition, the piece on audio formats at the end of this chapter can also explain a few questions some of you might have on that topic.

Because this comes from a blog (with a few minor tweak), I've left in most of the links in the digital versions of this document. Obviously, if you are reading a print version of this book, hyperlinks won't help much. For you, I've put all the links in this article at http://h2plink.com/AuphonicArticleLinks.

After recording a podcast or speech audio, it is usually necessary to modify the recorded levels. This post illustrates how to normalize the subjective loudness and how to compress the dynamic range (difference between the loudest and softest sounds) of an audio file.

Loudness normalization is one of the most common misunderstandings in audio post production. Many people use peak normalization, which ensures that the maximum peak (the maximum value of the audio data) reaches a specific level. However, the human perception of loudness does NOT depend on peak levels, therefore peak normalization is mostly useless. Recordings should be normalized according to its loudness, and not its peak level.

The correct calculation of the perceived loudness is actually not that easy, because psychoacoustic properties of human perception must be considered. A very rough approximation is the RMS value (short time quadratic mean of audio data), or even better: use your ears!

There are several reasons for loudness normalization and compression:

1. Mid-term loudness:

2. Different speakers or different regions in a recording might have very unequal loudness levels (e.g. a question from the audience at a conference). The audio engineer should balance the loudness of unequal parts, so that a listener doesn't have to adjust the volume all the time.

3. Short-term loudness:

4. Speech has a very high dynamic range, it consists of very quiet and very loud parts. However, when listening to podcasts on a portable player, in a car or even in the living room, a more uniform volume is

preferred, otherwise consonants like "p", "t" or a burst of laughter might be painful for your ears. Dynamic range compression (compressors) should be used to make the loud parts more quiet and the quiet parts louder.

5. Global Loudness:

6. The overall loudness of your recording should be comparable to previous episodes, to similar podcasts, to radio shows etc.

7. Peak Levels:

8. In digital recordings, the maximum peak level must not be louder than the maximum allowed level, otherwise an awful distortion called clipping occurs. Therefore one must ensure that all peaks are under a specific threshold.

In the following I will briefly describe how to adjust your peak levels, the mid-term, short-term and global loudness. The last section presents practical and detailed instructions, how all steps can be reproduced with the open source audio editor Audacity and some free plugins for Linux, Windows and Mac.1. Mid-Term: Loudness Normalization

The loudness of different regions in a recording should be unified, so that a listener doesn't have to adjust the volume all the time.

In live recordings this is often done by a sound engineer, using the faders of an audio mixer. She/he just listens to the signal and tries to keep a constant loudness. If the volume of a speaker is too low, the engineer will move the faders up and therefore increases the volume. However, an engineer must react fast enough on volume changes.

In post production, one can use volume envelopes to simulate the same behavior in a digital audio editor. The following picture shows volume envelope curves in Audacity:

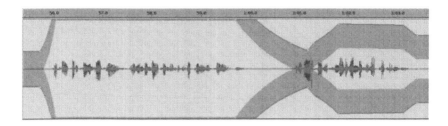

Using volume envelopes it is possible to amplify or lower the volume of different regions and speakers, so that in the end all parts have a similar loudness. This has the advantage, that volume fades can be positioned in an optimal way, but it might be a time consuming process if you are not used to it.

Additionally one should take care that background noises or e.g. loud breathing of speakers are not amplified too much.

2. Short-Term: Loudness Range Compression

A compressor reduces the volume of short and loud spikes (consonants like "p", "t", or laughter) and the output audio will have a more uniform loudness. All sounds with levels above the threshold will be reduced. The amount of gain reduction is determined by the ratio: e.g. if the ratio is 2:1 and the input level is 2dB over the threshold, the output level will be just 1dB over the threshold.

The following picture illustrates threshold and ratio (picture from MediaCollege):

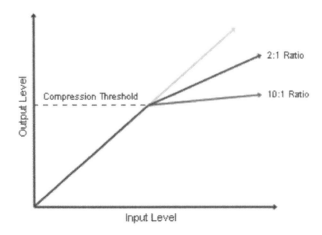

The threshold should be located above the average loudness of your recording, but below the volume of very loud spikes. For example, if the average level is -20dB, the threshold might be in the range of -16dB to -12dB, depending on the loudness range of the material.

Other compressor parameters can be set to standard values for speech, e.g. ratio = 5:1, attack = 5ms, release = 120ms. Feel free to experiment!

3. Global Level Adjustment

Now one should compare the loudness of the normalized audio

file to the loudness of other recordings like similar podcasts or radio shows. Raise or lower your volume, until the levels are similar. After doing this a few times, you will have a reference audio file (maybe one of your old shows) and can compare new recordings just to that one file.

Until recently, there was no standard way to measure the perceived loudness of sound recordings. Instead, audio productions were (and still are) normalized to peak levels, which do not determine how loud a signal is. Now we have the EBU recommendation R128 - a new and open standard for balancing audio programs according to their actually perceived loudness.

See the entire article at our blogpost at
http://h2plink.com/EBUR128.

4. Peak Limiting

The final step is the peak limiter. It ensures that the maximum audio peak level is small enough, so that no clipping or distortion is possible. You should keep your peaks at least below -1 dBFS, some suggest much more (-3dBFS, -6dBFS, ...).

That's because true peaks are often between samples (intersample peaks) and data compression algorithms (MP3, OGG, AAC, ...) produce artifacts at high peak levels.

Tools

All necessary operations should be possible with any modern

audio editor.

In the following I will describe how to reproduce all steps with the free and open source audio editor Audacity. Some LADSPA audio plugins are also required, because the current version of Audacity does not include a sufficient compressor and limiter.

On Windows or Mac install the LADSPA plugins bundle as described at http://h2plink.com/AudacityPlugins. On Linux install the swh-plugins (apt-get install swh-plugins on Ubuntu/Debian).

- Volume Envelopes:

- Select the Envelope Tool from the Tools Toolbar, for more information see Using the Envelope Tool or Audacity Manual Envelope Tool.

- Loudness Measurement (optional):

- You can use the Contrast Tool to calculate the average level (under Analyze -> Contrast). Select your audio and measure the volume, then you get a value in dB. This might help you while searching for the right compressor threshold.

- Compressor:

- A good compressor is the SC4 (or SC4 mono) compressor by Steve Harris (LADSPA plugin), you find it somewhere in Effects -> Plugins.

- Set the threshold as described above and the other parameters to e.g. ratio = 1:5, attack = 5ms, release = 120ms, knee = 3.5dB, RMS/peak = 0, makeup gain = 0dB.

- Level Adjustment:

- For global level adjustments you can use Effects -> Amplify (allow clipping, we have a limiter afterwards) or the gain control from the control panel of the audio track.

- Peak Limiter:

- Use the Fast Lookahead Limiter by Steve Harris (LADSPA plugin), you find it in Effects -> Plugins. Set the limit to -1dB or lower, input gain to 0dB and the release time to e.g. 0.12 seconds.

Another interesting tool is the Levelator (h2plink.com/Levelator). It tries to automate all the discussed steps and does it very nice. So if you just want to throw your audio in and get it back with good levels, use this program.

But be careful, it might produce common artifacts like pumping and also amplifies unwanted sounds like breathing, background noises, etc.

Summary

I hope you are convinced now that peak normalization is not

the same as loudness normalization and should be avoided.

A detailed loudness post production of podcasts or speech audio should involve the following step:

1. Loudness normalization: Bring different parts to a uniform volume.

2. Dynamic range compression: Use a compressor to lower the volume of short and loud spikes.

3. Global volume adaptation: Raise or lower the volume of the whole audio file to a similar loudness level than other programs.

4. Peak limiter: Limit all peaks to at least -1dBFS to avoid clipping.

Audio File Formats for Podcasts

Many different audio file formats exist for storing recorded audio data on a computer system. This post compares various types and gives suggestions on which format one should use, especially when producing podcasts or other online audio.

If you just want to see some practical tips, skip the description and just read the conclusion.

There are three main types of audio file formats:

1. Uncompressed audio formats:

2. Uncompressed audio formats store the audio information as it is recorded. This results in big files, but no information is lost, therefore they are suitable for archiving original recordings. The most common uncompressed audio format is PCM, which is usually stored in a WAV or AIFF file.

3. Lossless compression:

4. Lossless audio compression formats need less space than uncompressed formats, without any loss in quality. They work similar to ZIP, but the compression algorithms are specifically designed for audio data. Some example formats are FLAC (Free Lossless Audio Codec) or ALAC (Apple Lossless Audio Codec), for a comparison of various codecs see Lossless comparison.

5. Lossy compression:

6. Lossy compression formats significantly reduce the file size, by throwing away information imperceptible to humans. This gives very small files, but some information is lost and cannot be reconstructed. The best-known example is MP3, others are Ogg Vorbis, AAC,WMA...

A great source of information about audio codecs and listening tests is the Hydrogen Audio wiki and forum (http://h2plink.com/HydrogenAudio).

Relevant Audio Formats for Podcasts

When distributing a podcast or other audio over the internet, you want to have the smallest possible file size, the best possible quality and everyone should be able to play it (on all operating systems, on mobile phones, portable audio players, car audio players etc.).

Because of the much smaller file size, lossy formats are the only real option. Additionally one may archive the produced podcast in an uncompressed or lossless compressed audio file.

The characteristics of a few important formats are listed below.

MP3: MPEG-1 Audio Layer 3 (description)

- the most widespread and the de facto standard of online audio file formats

- most, if not all, hardware players support MP3

- acceptable quality, but already quite old

- patented: a license is required to "distribute and/or sell decoders and/or encoders" (see http://h2plink.com/mp3License for more on MP3 licensing and patent issues)

Ogg Vorbis:

- an open source and patent free audio codec

- performs very well from low to high bitrates (more

advanced than MP3)

- widespread in the open source community

- some implementations are more computationally intensive than MP3

- some portable players support Ogg Vorbis out of the box (see http://h2plink.com/VorbisPortablePlayers)

AAC: Advanced Audio Codec (http://h2plink.com/AAC)

- the latest industry standard and the official successor to MP3 (also called MP4 audio, most common file extension is M4A)

- different types of AAC exist (LC AAC, HE AAC, HE AAC v2)

- the AAC format is on par with Ogg Vorbis and other modern codecs, HE AAC should provide higher quality at low bitrates

- HE AAC uses spectral band replication (high frequencies are removed and calculated from lower frequencies, see SBR), HE AAC v2 adds a parametric stereo method (stereo audio is created out of a mono signal, see PS) - don't use HE AAC for higher bitrates!

- heavily patented: a patent license is required for all manufacturers or developers of AAC codecs

- widespread in the apple community (iTunes, iPod, iPhones etc.), many other portable players don't support AAC

FLAC: Free Lossless Audio Codec (http://h2plink.com/FLAC)

- lossless compression, no information is lost

- flac files are typically reduced to 40-60% of their original size

- very fast encoding and decoding

- open source and patent free

OPUS: The Open Audio Codec For Podcasts And Internet Audio (http://h2plink.com/Opus)

- suitability for both, music and speech

- outstanding sound quality at also very low bitrates.

For a detailed comparison of various codecs at different bitrates see http://h2plink.com/Codec.

Conclusion

If you want to reach everyone and maintain only one file format, you have only one choice: MP3. It is not the most advanced codec, but everything supports it and the quality is sufficient.

Additionally it may be advantageous to offer your audio in Ogg

Vorbis or AAC. Ogg Vorbis is widespread in the open source and creative commons movement (http://h2plink.com/CreativeCommons) and should be used when patent problems are important for you. AAC is the new standard on all "i"-Devices (Apple) and shows very good performance especially at low bitrates (HE AAC).

Finally, if you also want to archive an original version of your audio, use FLAC or just PCM (WAV, AIFF).

Can You Talk (With Dave Jackson)?

Dave Jackson is a great friend has been running the School Of Podcasting (http://h2plink.com/SOP) for what seems like forever. He's stayed true to the space and has helped a lot of people get their podcast running over the last decade. A lot of people have asked Dave if podcasting is for them and he's always pointed them in the right direction. Dave gets technical when he needs to, but always keeps a teacher's heart.

Can you podcast? You might be thinking, "NO, I'm not a "technical person." To this I ask:

Can you talk?

Can you attach a picture to an email?

Can you upload a picture to Facebook?

Have you ever used a word processor like Microsoft Word?

When you're in the car (or at home) and the phone rings, do you turn down the radio/tv so you can talk?

If you answered yes to the above you can podcast. Let me explain:

1. You need to know how to talk. You don't need a giant voice, you just need to talk.

2. Uploading a picture to facebook or attaching a file to email is the exact same process as uploading a file to a media host, or uploading an image to a post.

3. If you have ever used a program like Microsoft Word, then using a program like WordPress is not that different. I'm not going to lie, there is a learning curve, but I could explain the difference in about 15 minutes. It's a very short learning curve.

4. You might say, "I don't know anything about mixing audio - but when you turn the radio down in the car so you can talk on the phone you "mixed" audio levels. Mixing is simply adjusting audio to the proper levels to provide the best result.

In general human beings don't like change. They don't like new. That's normal. Embrace your nervousness, get a microphone and press record.

Make Digital Media

If you are on a tight budget, you can purchase the Audio Technica ATR2100usb microphone for around $60, plug it into your computer. Use a free program called Audacity, and press the big red record button. It's pretty much that easy. Recording is easy, but creating content is not.

You can record audio, or you can make content. There is a difference.

Audio is two dudes popping some brews and chewing the fat.

Content is two dudes, popping some brews, and bringing value to their audience.

169

Before you plug in that ATR2100, you need to ask yourself these questions

What do I want my audience to do with this?

How will this move them?

You want you content to make them: laugh, cry, think, groan, (or educate /entertain them).

Audio:

I had a salad for dinner.

Content:

I had a salad for dinner and accidentally swallowed ¼ of a tomatoes that got stuck in my throat. I could breathe through my nose but not swallow. All of the typical things you do to help someone choking did not have any success. . I would try to drink water, and it would go down my throat and then right back up. In the end, I went to the emergency room. Upon arrival, I relaxed. That relaxation allowed allowed the tomato to slide down my throat.

In the book *Secrets of Dynamic Communication,* Ken Davis advises people to boil their presentation down to one point. My one point for my podcast might be; "When you find yourself in a stressful situation, one the best things you can do is take a deep breath and try to relax." Then I could use that story to illustrate my point.

Recording audio is easy.

Creating content takes some time and thought.

Don't make audio. Make content instead.

Dave Jackson founded the School of Podcasting in 2005 where he has helped hundreds of people launch podcasts that impact their audience. He is also the author of the books *More Podcast Money, and My Favorite Podcast is...* and he is the Director of Podcasting for the New Media Expo. You can find Dave at http://h2plink.com/SOP.

Podcasting: Part of a Multicast Marketing Strategy (With Gary Leland)

Gary is a hero of mine. He's been a part of the podcasting game pretty much since day one and his business leadership has been an inspiration to me in ways he'll never know. Gary is having a ton of fun, but still making some serious coin along the way - two goals I share

And, yes, he is the Gary Leland of "Podcast Pickle" fame.

What exactly is Multicasting? I define multicasting as taking one piece of content and distributing it to as many places, formats, and devices as possible.

In this chapter, I am going to start with a video interview I recently recorded. I will show you how to use the content in this video and distribute it as video, audio, and text.

Distributing the interview in different formats will allow people to see the content where they are, and in the format they prefer, instead of asking them to come to where the content is. In other words, put your content everywhere.

As the topic of this chapter states I start with a podcast, and in my case a video podcast. To make it easy for you, I will break this down into three parts: video, audio, and text. If you do not have a video podcast at this time, you may want to start with the audio section.

Video: I start with The Fastpitch TV Show

1. I upload my video to Libsyn.com to create my podcast, but there are several options for uploading your podcast episodes, such as Blubrry.com and others

2. When I upload my video to Libsyn, it automatically uploads to iTunes for people using Apple devices. https://itunes.apple.com/us/podcast/fastpitch-softball-tv-show/id274993094?mt=2&uo=4&at=10laQs

3. When I upload my video to Libsyn, it automatically uploads to Stitcher.com for people using Android devices, but it uploads the audio only. http://www.stitcher.com/podcast/fastpitch-chat/fastpitch-softball-show?refid=stpr

4. I upload my video to Youtube.com https://www.youtube.com/watch?v=Ibv8dKLTZvw&index=2&list=PLgXFT8-8dStq00XANDDF9bZVJzZk3nFPe

5. I add my video to my blog http://fastpitch.tv/jennie-finch-interview

6. I upload my video to Vimeo https://vimeo.com/114905831

7. I add the video to my online magazine http://fastpitch.tv/category/fastpitch-softball-magazine

8. My video is automatically uploaded to my iPhone and Android App when I upload to Libsyn.com https://itunes.apple.com/us/app/fastpitch-softball-tv/id333245873?mt=8&ign-mpt=uo%3D4

9. I upload my video file to Facebook. I do not mean I add a link to my show. I actually upload it to Facebook. https://www.facebook.com/video.php?v=2686662478280&set=vl.693830830734640&type=2&theater

Audio: I pull the audio out of my video and create a new version of the show just for audio listeners.

This is The Fastpitch Radio Show

10. I upload my audio to Libsyn.com to create my podcast

11. When I upload my audio to Libsyn, it automatically uploads to iTunes for people using Apple devices. https://itunes.apple.com/us/podcast/fastpitch-softball-radio-network/id273121222?mt=2&ign-mpt=uo%3D4

12. When I upload my audio to Libsyn it automatically uploads to Stitcher.com for people using Android devices http://www.stitcher.com/podcast/fastpitch-chat/fastpitch-radio-show?refid=stpr

13. I add the audio to my blog http://fastpitch.tv/jennie-finch-interview-2

14. When I upload my audio to Libsyn, it automatically uploads to my iTunes and Android Apps. https://itunes.apple.com/us/app/fastpitch-radio-show/id365526757?mt=8&ign-mpt=uo%3D4

Text: I transcribe the audio to text

15. I upload on the Fastpitch Blog http://fastpitch.tv/jennie-finc-questions

16. I make a slide share presentation http://www.slideshare.net/GaryLeland/finch-

slideshare?qid=c35ce260-07e9-4806-bce3-
477f2f408e5d&v=default&b=&from_search=1

17. I compile many interviews and create an ebook.
http://fastpitch.tv/publishing

18. I give away a free copy of my ebook to people who
subscribe to my newsletter.
http://fastpitch.tv/newsletter

20. Create a paperback version of your book.
https://www.createspace.com/

21. By using rss feeds, all of my content automatically
distributes to my Tumbler Page
http://planetsoftball.com/

22. My RSS feed also distributes to Paper.Li
https://paper.li/f-1414789585

This was just a small sampling of the methods you can use and
reuse the same content over and over. By mixing this content
in with your new content you can give yourself the appearance
of having more content than you actually produce. Most users
will find their favorite method of absorbing your content and
go with that.You may want to spread some of the distribution
out over time, so it appears fresh to your audience.

Gary leland started his first retail store in 1979, his first e-
commerce site in 1996, and his first podcast in 2004. In 2006
Time Magazine included his podcasting website in their 50
coolest websites of the year. Today Gary spends most of his
time running the Fastpitch TV Network, but still dabbles in the

podcasting world as a Founder of Podcast Movement and the Publisher of Podertainment, the podcast magazine.

More Than One Way To Record A Podcast (With Chris Chrisensen)

Chris is one of the good guys and has been doing this for a long time. He is friend and inspiration. I'm thrilled to be able to share him with you.

Like skinning a cat, there is more than one way to record a podcast. I produce three audio podcasts and the occasional video podcast episode. In total, I have recorded over 1,000 episodes. Each podcast I record uses a slightly different procedure.

Podcast: Amateur Traveler

Downloads per year: 1.3 million

Style: Interview

Summary: Highlights a new travel destination each week

Started: July 2005

Episodes: 452 episodes, produced weekly

Production: Eight hours a week (Five hours outsourced)

Duration: 45 minutes

This award winning podcast gets me invited to trips around the world so it is worth putting both my time into and the time of an external editor. Because this show is talking about destinations, the episodes have lasting value. Roughly half of podcasts downloaded in any given month will be for older episodes. The podcast that I have produced the longest is the Amateur Traveler.

I produce this show as an iTunes Enhanced Podcast. In addition to an mp3 version of the show, there is also a version that has photos and links related to the topic my guest and I are discussing. Production of an iTunes Enhanced Podcast must use Apple's Garageband software and can only be listened to on an Apple device. Apple seems less committed to this format these days so I do not know that I would recommend this path if you are just starting out.

Process:

1. My guest and I connect on Skype. I use Skype on a computer or a smart phone because of the difference in audio quality between Skype and a landline. I have always had a no cell phone rule for guests.

2. I record the call with CallRecorder on a Mac. CallRecorder is configured to automatically record all my calls to avoid those embarrassing "oops, I didn't hit record" conversations.

3. I convert the CallRecorder files from movie files to .aif files with me on one channel and my guest on the other. I do this using tools provided by CallRecorder. I drop both tracks into a GarageBand file and then compress this file and put it into DropBox for my editor.

4. My editor edits this file to take out some of the rough edges, long pauses when someone has to look up what the name of that great restaurant was,flubs. He then makes a second pass through the file to put in photos

and links that match what we are talking about which he also adds to a list of links that he uses for the show notes. When he is done, he drops that file in a different DropBox folder for me.

5. I make sure the file transferred correctly and pay my editor $60 for the roughly five hours he spent.

6. I record the intro, and sponsorship ads, a news segment, news from the community and the closing.

7. I listen to the first part of the show again and compose show notes with all the links from my editor, a description of the show, links for the news stories and community news. I also add in the ads to the show notes.

8. I create both the mp3 and iTunes Enhanced versions (aac) version of the show

9. I copy my show notes to the "lyrics" section of iTunes, and update any other fields that are relevant.

10. I upload the files to libsyn.com and place the link to the audio player in the show notes

11. I publish and celebrate that I have gone one more week without podfading

Challenges:

1. Some shows do not work. Not everyone I interview

results in a show worth using. I need to stay a couple of weeks ahead of release with interviews to maintain the quality of my show.

2. As with all interview shows, scheduling is a pain.

3. This is a crazy amount of work. I would have quit a few years back if I had not outsourced the bulk of the editing.

Podcast: The Bible Study Podcast

Downloads per year: 200,000

Style: monologue

Summary: All of the bible but with none of the politics

Started: October 2006

Episodes: 388 weekly episodes

Production: < 1 hour

Duration: 10 minutes

When I originally thought about podcasting one of the shows I considered was a religious show because I love to teach. Like so many podcasters I thought, well if I can do one I can certainly do two. Of course, when I started this show Amateur Traveler was unedited, so it did not take as much time.

Process:

1. Turn on Garageband and start talking. I do this show without a script so the raw audio is a mess.

2. Edit in Garageband, publish mp3 to iTunes

3. Sketch brief show notes including a link to the chapter of the bible covered

4. Set the lyrics of the mp3 file to the text of the bible covered

5. Upload the files to libsyn.com and place the link to the audio player in the show notes

6. Publish and relax

Challenges:

1. Almost none. I can record this anywhere I have a microphone and often edit it on a commuter train. There are easy ways to podcast and while this is not the easiest. It is far from the hardest.

Podcast: This Week in Travel

Downloads per year: 100,000

Style: Four person round table discussion, Google+ hangout

Summary: A comedy show about travel or a serious show about travel news, depending on the week

Started: August 2009

Episodes: 181 episodes, produced roughly every other week

Production: Two hours a week

Duration: 60 minutes

In 2009, I met Gary Arndt and Jen Leo at a Travel Blogger's conference and Gary pitched the idea of doing a weekly podcast. The idea was to have a four person round table discussion with three regular hosts and one or two guests. The goal of this show was to establish more links to traditional travel writers and editors who Jen knew. Gary and I have won travel awards from traditional travel journalism organizations since we started this show and part of the reason was the visibility it gave us.

I knew I could not do the same kind of production for this show on top of two other podcasts. Editing a four person discussion is harder, so this show is almost completely unedited.

We originally recorded This Week in Travel on Skype but it is now recorded as a Google+ Hangout.

Process:

1. Connect with everyone on Google+ using Hangouts on the Air. This step will take some time if the guest is not familiar with this system. Be prepared for some explanation and troubleshooting before recording. pa

2. Press record, talk for an hour, Press stop

3. Google publishes straight to YouTube. Update the show with information on YouTube. If we did not want an audio version, we would be done at this point, but we would not have a podcast. Also we would be giving up 95% of our audience.

4. Go to the YouTube Channel Manager and download the video file

5. Open the video file in Quicktime and convert to an audio file, use iTunes to convert that audio file to mp3

6. Write the show notes including links to the stories we talked about and the video player

7. Set the lyrics of the mp3 file to a version of the show notes, update all the other fields in iTunes

8. Upload the files to libsyn.com and place the link to the audio player in the show notes

9. Publish and celebrate that this week there is a This Week in Travel

Challenges:

1. Because we are on video we need better internet connections. This is challenging because we do a travel show and have recorded with all four people on different continents.

2. If you think scheduling a four person show seems like an issue throw in bad hotel internet, and someone taking a trip somewhere virtually every week.

Conclusion:

There is more than one way to create the audio for a podcast.

Some ways produce higher quality audio. Some ways take less time. The needs of the podcaster, the preferences of the audience and the goal of the podcast all factor into what method is right for your next show.

Tell the World

Recording a podcast can be enjoyable, but many of the benefits of podcasting get better if more people listen. Other than hoping that iTunes will drop listeners at your door, what can you do?

Let us assume you are recording a podcast that has some value. It teaches something or it provides entertainment. Then somewhere out there may be two different groups of people:

People who want to listen to what you have created

People, besides you, who benefit from your podcast getting heard

To find the people in group one we pass out copies of the podcast, wear podcast branded t-shirts, make sure the SEO for our website is good and that we have good show notes possibly even a transcript. We submit press releases, buy advertising, build twitter followings and pin it to Pinterest. We talk about the podcast to our friends, get speaking engagements, pray for "New and Notable", sacrifice the blood of a chicken and hope to get on Oprah.

But what about the other group? Who else, besides your sponsors, would benefit from your podcast getting heard and how can you recruit their help?

My main podcast, Amateur Traveler (http://AmateurTraveler.com), is a podcast about travel destinations. Each week we talk about some city or country. We cover everything from what to put on your Chicago dog in the Windy City to going to Tonga and swimming with whales.

Almost all of these destinations have a group of people who are paid to professionally promote that destination; such as a Tourism Board, a CVB (Convention and Visitors Bureau), a DMO (Destination Marketing Organization). So, every time I produce a podcast I send an email to the DMO. I do not just tweet, but I send a tweet to the DMO. Is there a national airline that flies to that country? I copy them as well. I email them, including the HTML for a player (most don't use it) and a media kit about Amateur Traveler (http://AmateurTraveler.com/MediaKit.pdf). Most podcasters do not link to the show but a few do. But most will at least promote the show on Twitter, Facebook, Google+ or whatever they use for social media.

Moreover, Amateur Traveler is an interview show. Most weeks the person I am interviewing also has a blog or a website or a social media following. I send the guest a player to the show to put on their site, which many post. The HTML I send them has a link to my website for the show notes which helps my site get more search engine traffic. Why do they do this? I just introduced them to 10,000 people who like travel. That is not bad for them either. We edit the show so that they sound good. Robert Reid from National Geographic said his favorite interview he ever did was for Amateur Traveler on his home state of Oklahoma. So, guests almost always at least promote the show on social media.

Promotion does not have to stop the week the podcast comes out. I have over nine years of content and republish six old posts everyday, making sure to copy the DMO or the guest as appropriate.

My son Mike and a co-host Jay have started a new Comics podcast called Because Comics

(http://www.partialarc.com/because-comics/). They do not do an interview and don't talk about travel. But, there are still people who would be interested in their show and people who will benefit from the show being heard.

The latest episode of Because Comics:

Both Jay and Mike each talked about one new comic they have read, their "pull list". This episode talked about a new take on "Batgirl" and on "Storm" from the "X-Men" universe.

The main segment about a crossover comics when "Archie" meets "Glee" (Not quite as weird as the episode when "Archie" met the "Punisher").

A game segment where they talked about which superhero would be the best or worst at a mundane job (called "Super Mundane") where they debated the merits of Captain Marvel vs the Flash as babysitters.

So, first, who would be interested in hearing this show? They have opportunities to reach out to the fans of "Batgirl", "X-Men", "Archie", "Glee" and the "Flash" at least, as well as people who love comics. So does the TV show Flash have an account on twitter? Where do lovers of Glee hang out? What hashtags do people who read Archie use? Are there celebrities that are affiliated with any of those groups? How about tweeting the actor who plays the Flash the conclusion that the Flash might be a great babysitter? What about a warning to an actress on Glee of what not to do should their world collide with the Archie Universe?

Who else would benefit from this show being heard? Well certainly the publishers of the two new comic books, but also all the publishers and related TV and movie brands. Who handles their publicity? What are their social media accounts?

How about your show? What's your next step?

When not hosting travel podcasts, Chris Christensen has worked for years in technology startups in Silicon Valley. He was formerly the Director of Engineering for TripAdvisor's New Initiatives group, the EVP Engineering at LiveWorld, where his team built and ran online communities and events for eBay, HBO, TV Guide, Expedia, Marriott, A&E, History Channel, the NBA, NBC, ABC, Disney, Microsoft, WebTV and American Express. Chris now owns and runs BloggerBridge.com which is a new startup connecting bloggers and industry contacts.

PART 3 - FREE VIDEOS AND PODCASTS I LISTEN TO

About Your Free Videos

As I wrote this book, I knew there would be times when something would be better presented in video format than the written word. I have no problem with that - so here is a list of all of the videos referred to in this book and the H2P link for each allowing me to update them if/when needed.

I would bet good money (and this isn't my first book) that I'll be adding some additional videos to this batch. If you register your book (http://www.howToPodcastbook.com/Register), I'll let you know when I do - and I'll let you know if I/when release any updates to the ones listed below.

With that said and done, here are the videos ...

Make Digital Media

How To Record Audio On Your iPhone Or Android Device With The iRig Mic Cast

http://h2plink.com/AudioOnMicCast

How To Record And Edit Audio On Your Computer With Audacity And The Nessie USB Microphone

http://h2plink.com/AudacityNessie

How I Record "Thinking Out Loud" Using Nothing But My iPhone

http://h2plink.com/HowIRecordTOL

How I Optimize My Audio And Convert It To MP3 Using Auphonic

http://h2plink.com/AuphonicVIdeo

Put It Online

Quick Examples Of Putting Podcast Media Online

http://h2plink.com/PutMediaOnline

Make It Podcast Ready

How To Check If Your Podcast Feed "Works"
http://h2plink.com/iTunesCheck

How A Podcast Host Makes My RSS So I Don't Have To
http://h2plink.com/MakesMyRSS

Tell The World

How To Submit Your Podcast To iTunes

http://h2plink.com/SubmitToItunes

Podcasts I Listen To

I'm always asked about which podcasts I listen to. While my job takes me all over the place and has me listening to a lot more podcasts than would be recommended, these are the shows I consume on a regular basis. I think you might enjoy them and I believe they have something to teach you about podcasting. I present them in alphabetical order, simply so as not to make you think I prefer one over the other.

10x Talks (http://h2plink.com/10xTalks)

Full disclosure: this one is a client of mine, but honestly, I'd be listening to this show even if I wasn't paid to do so. Joe Polish (of *I Love Marketing*, also on this list) and Dan Sullivan discuss life for the entrepreneur. Unlike some of the more exploratory podcasts where participants work out together what they're thinking, this show is truly two masters in their game teaching each other - and their listeners - about what really matters. Sullivan keeps a focus and attention on this show which almost all podcasters can learn from.

Back To Work (http://h2plink.com/5b5b2w)

From their website (at least at the time of publication): "***Back to Work*** is an award-winning talk show with Merlin Mann and Dan Benjamin discussing productivity, communication, work, barriers, constraints, tools and more." Dan Benjamin is also on this list with **Podcast Method** and Merlin Mann is a long-time figure in the productivity space. Dan and Merlin get together weekly to simply work through life and productivity and cover topics ranging from everything listed in the official description to hour-long rants about comic books, aspects of nerd culture and more. They are certainly an acquired taste, but once you are hooked, you'll never go back. The joke is, no one expected them to pass three episodes... as I write this, they have passed the 200 mark and I haven't missed a single one.

Entreleadership (http://h2plink.com/Entreleadership)

Financial guru and radio personality Dave Ramsey has an entire company dedicated to leadership in the entrepreneurial space, a topic near to my heart. This particular show is a promotional element for his programs which provides a perfect example of the integrated approach to podcast monetization that I'm frequently asked to speak and write about. The quality of interviewees his team is able to get, combined with snippets from Dave himself, make this a must-listen-to podcast, even if it wasn't such a great example of how to run one.

I Love Marketing (http://h2plink.com/ILoveMarketing)

As with **10xTalks**, this is a client of mine - so I should disclose that as I write this. With that said and done, this format of two geniuses, completely unleashed, sharing their knowledge and rolodex with anyone who will listen is in many ways the marketing degree I never got. There is honestly a lot to complain about when it comes to this podcast - sound quality is varied, focus is sometimes non-existent and the degree of wasted time in host banter has turned away some. But, despite all this, there is something extremely magnetic about these two hosts and the wisdom one can glean from a mere 10-

minute segment of each program. It's almost always been worth more than the price of admission. This is one of those productions that could only exist as a podcast - and I'm thrilled that it does. Their download numbers prove that I'm not the only one who likes it.

Mac Power Users Podcast
(http://h2plink.com/MacPowerUsers)

This is another of those shows which could only exist in podcast form, and that's part of why I love it. Mac über-enthusiasts Katie Floyd and David Sparks hit topics related to Mac and iOS devices that are so in-depth, you walk away feeling like you actually understand every single element of what is at play. The content could be too technical for some, but for those passionate about tech, it's always a fun listen.

Marketing Over Coffee (http://h2plink.com/MOC)

This one has been around for a long time but continues to be a mainstay worth listening to every week. John Wall and Christopher Penn hit topics of marketing in the news and share what they think and what they're doing about it. On occasion, they interview some of the top names in online marketing - but do so with an intimacy on the topics which lets them go deeper than you'd usually expect.

Online Marketing Made Easy (http://h2plink.com/Amy)

When my dear friend Amy Porterfield (don't miss her bonus chapter in this book) launched her podcast, I knew it was going to be good. I didn't expect it would be the smash hit that it is, but Amy does nothing other than continue to surprise and rise up the charts. Amy is so giving in her content that you might wonder what's left in her premium offerings; but don't worry, there is plenty. This show feels like a ton of work goes into each and every episode and I've never walked away from an episode without at least one actionable item that has made my business better.

Podcast Method (http://h2plink.com/PodcastMethod)

Dan Benjamin (mentioned earlier in this piece) recently started this podcast about podcasting methods, and although he and I differ greatly on some topics and approaches, his absolute professionalism in everything he does is an inspiration and worth striving to emulate. I don't know how long this one will go on for - but do go back and listen to the archives, even if he never does another one. As my goal for this book has always been to make your podcast journey simple, I should point out that he goes in-depth with every topic he takes on. He could steer you in directions that might take days (or even weeks) of your life, but if you go in that direction, I could imagine no better guide.

School Of Podcasting (http://h2plink.com/DavidSOP)

David Jackson is one of the good guys and has been in podcasting nearly since day one. His membership site (don't forget to read his bonus chapter and see the crazy bonus offer he's made to my readers) has been a staple in teaching others how to podcast. I have sent more people there than all of the other how-to-podcast sites and programs combined. Since the beginning, his free show continues to point us all in the right direction. I can't say I've caught every single one of his 400-plus episodes, but every one I've heard has pointed me in the direction of being a better podcaster.

Startup (http://h2plink.com/StartupPodcast)

Startup is a show about a startup (hence the name) that, funnily enough, happens to be a podcast company. It is as meta as things get... and I love it. It's produced by Alex Blumberg, who came from public radio, so he brings a combined passion and professionalism to this space that is greatly needed. Lessons learned from this podcast will be something I examine in detail in an upcoming episode of *The Podcast Report*.

Tim Ferriss Show (http://h2plink.com/TimFerriss). Tim Ferriss of *The 4-Hour Workweek* and *4-Hour Body* fame jumped into podcasting full-on and hasn't looked back; he doesn't know how to do things any other way. The access Tim has to fascinating people and the way his mind works makes every episode a home run. His focus is the content and he communicates it well.

The Podcast Report
(http://h2plink.com/ThePodcastReport). Of course I listen to this one - as it's mine. I hope you might listen too!

Register For More!

It doesn't have to end here ...

For everyone who registers this book:

- updates on the content

- access to the more than $900 worth of bonuses (while supplies last)

- additional podcast training videos

- material we couldn't fit in the book

- surprise bonuses

- exclusive discounts

- and more

http://HowToPodcastBook.com/Register

Printed in Great Britain
by Amazon